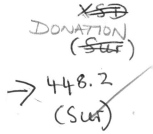

DONATION (SLF)

→ 448.2 (Suf)

Le ou La?

1853592682

MODERN LANGUAGES IN PRACTICE

Series Editor
Michael Grenfell, *School of Education, University of Southampton*

Editorial Board
Do Coyle, *School of Education, University of Nottingham*
Simon Green, *Trinity & All Saints College, Leeds*

Editorial Consultant
Christopher Brumfit, *Centre for Language in Education, University of Southampton*

Other Books of Interest
Approaches to Second Language Acquisition
    R. TOWELL and R. HAWKINS
Fluency and Accuracy
    HECTOR HAMMERLY
Foundations of Bilingual Education and Bilingualism
    COLIN BAKER
French for Communication 1979-1990
    ROY DUNNING
Investigating Cultural Studies in Foreign Language Teaching
    M. BYRAM and V. ESARTE-SARRIES
Life in Language Immersion Classrooms
    ELIZABETH B. BERNHARDT (ed.)
Quantifying Language
    PHIL SCHOLFIELD
Reflections on Language Learning
    L. BARBARA and M. SCOTT (eds)
Second Language Acquisition and Language Pedagogy
    ROD ELLIS
Tasks and Language Learning
    GRAHAM CROOKES and SUSAN M. GASS (eds)
Tasks in a Pedagogical Context
    GRAHAM CROOKES and SUSAN M. GASS (eds)
Teaching-and-Learning Language-and-Culture
    MICHAEL BYRAM, CAROL MORGAN and colleagues

Please contact us for the latest book information:
Multilingual Matters Ltd,
Frankfurt Lodge, Clevedon Hall, Victoria Road,
Clevedon, Avon, England BS21 7SJ

MODERN LANGUAGES IN PRACTICE 1
Series Editor: Michael Grenfell

Le ou La?

The Gender of French Nouns

Marie Surridge

MULTILINGUAL MATTERS LTD
Clevedon • Philadelphia • Adelaide

Library of Congress Cataloging in Publication Data

Surridge, Marie, 1931-
Le ou La?: The Gender of French Nouns/Marie Surridge
(Modern Languages in Practice: 1)
Includes bibliographical references
1. French language–Gender. 2. French language–Nouns. I. Title. II. Series
PC2211.S97   1995
445-dc20   94-47319

British Library Cataloguing in Publication Data

A CIP catalogue record for this book is available from the British Library.

ISBN 1-85359-269-2 (hbk)
ISBN 1-85359-268-4 (pbk)

Multilingual Matters Ltd

UK: Frankfurt Lodge, Clevedon Hall, Victoria Road, Clevedon, Avon BS21 7SJ.
USA: 1900 Frost Road, Suite 101, Bristol, PA 19007, USA.
Australia: P.O. Box 6025, 83 Gilles Street, Adelaide, SA 5000, Australia.

Cartoons by Ron Hore
Cover design by Bob Jones Associates.
Printed and bound in Great Britain by WBC Ltd, Bridgend.

Contents

Foreword

This book is intended to help students of French as a second language to discover the systems at work in the assignment of noun genders in French, and to develop effective methods for assigning genders correctly. It is directed towards the serious student at intermediate level or above (post-GCSE in Britain). It should also be able to meet the needs of people using French as a second language at an otherwise highly competent level, including many possessing degrees in French, who find gender assignment to be a persistent, virtually intractable problem. This difficulty is particularly acute for those whose native language (for example, English) does not possess a rigorous system of noun classification like that of French. However, even those whose own language has a gender system somewhat similar to that of French (for example, German speakers) are not exempt.

Special difficulties arise from the fact that the rules governing gender assignment in French are far from obvious. For generations, it has been said that gender assignment for inanimate nouns in French is arbitrary, and that genders are learned word by word. This view would have us believe that gender is different from all other linguistic phenomena, which are universally thought to be rule-governed. In recent years, research has in fact shown that gender assignment in French depends on a network of systems, albeit a somewhat complex network.

Native speakers of French are now thought to internalise the various systems in stages, progressing from simple nouns (those containing only one meaningful element) through the different types of complex nouns (those with more than one such element). Students of French should ideally mimic this progression. It is, however, difficult for students of adult or near-adult age to do this while acquiring a functioning vocabulary appropriate to their needs. By dividing the chapters according to the type of words treated, I have tried to provide a substitute for the natural stratification without restricting students to a form of language incapable of expressing their interests. Those at the intermediate level could with profit work methodically through the book. Students who have reached a more advanced stage without dealing with the gender problem as they went along may want to give the book a first, rapid reading, with the object of obtaining a general overview, before starting to bring their gender competence slowly up to the general standard of their French by correcting one stratum of vocabulary at a time.

Examples are selected from vocabulary which should for the most part be familiar to intermediate students. The majority of words used are to be found in *le français fondamental*, which was designed to include many of the most common words in the language, or in vocabulary lists intended for students. Others are in everyday use in contemporary life, and are likely to be known to any student who has spent time in a Francophone environment. For this reason, words used as examples are not normally translated.

A Note on Technical Terms

As far as possible, technical terms are avoided in this book. To eliminate them altogether, however, would in some cases result in the use of repeated clumsy substitutes. I have compromised by inserting, at the first occurrence of any technical term, a lay person's paraphrase or, where necessary, a longer explanation. If the meaning of a term you have already encountered escapes you, the Index of Terms on the following page gives a reference taking you to the explanation in the text.

Index of Terms

The following list gives the page in the text on which each term is explained.

Introduction

First, what is gender? The simple answer is that it is the classification of nouns as masculine, feminine or neuter. In French, there is no neuter noun gender, so gender in French is the classification of nouns as masculine or feminine.

This definition would not help you much, however, if you did not know how gender affects the way in which nouns are used in French. You also need to know that gender is expressed by variations in the following:

the definite or indefinite articles, such as *le, la, un, une*;

pronouns and demonstrative adjectives linked to the noun, such as *il, elle, ce, cette, celui, celle*;

adjectives agreeing with the noun, either as part of the noun phrase (la *belle* ville) or following a verb, when it expresses an attribute of the noun (la ville est *belle*).

Items such as these, which indicate the gender of a noun, are called 'gender markers'.

Is there anyone who has managed to learn French as a second language without having great difficulty in getting the genders right? In a career devoted to teaching university students of French, I have never encountered any. In my experience, genders, together with the forms of verbs, are the most difficult part of starting to learn French seriously. But there is an important difference between the two phenomena: in time, most people are able to master the verbs, whereas it is exceedingly rare for them to eliminate defects in gender assignment (knowing which gender to use for a given noun). A study of fourth year university students in Canada in 1984 showed that on average they scored 83.5% in a test of gender assignment. At first sight, that might seem to be a fairly respectable score, but since the words used in the test were chosen from amongst the most frequent in French, the number of mistakes is hardly acceptable. Comments from teachers at all levels give no reason to believe that the grasp of genders is less tenuous in other countries. The gender problem is probably the most persistent one encountered by learners of French.

Unless errors of gender are virtually eliminated, such students will never achieve native-like competence in French: they will always mark themselves as outsiders *trying* to speak French. Worse, they will certainly be hampered in their efforts to communicate with Francophones. To the learner, a gender error seems like a tiny and unimportant mistake which will not affect the sense of the utterance. Yet, if you look closely at the reactions of Francophones to such mistakes, you will realise that the result is often total incomprehension. Try asking for 'une petite pain'. The listener may realise that you have made a gender error or, on the other hand, wonder what you mean by *pain* which, since you have made it feminine, simply cannot mean 'bread', 'roll' or 'bun'. We get the impression that, for the native speaker of French, the gender, far from being an insignificant accessory, is part and parcel of the noun. The behaviour of Francophone parents towards their children supports this view: they just do not tolerate incorrect genders.

Francophone children, once beyond babyhood, rarely make gender errors. It is particularly irritating for students of French to observe that tiny children only just able to form a sentence normally use the appropriate gender for a noun. In fact, however, students should take courage from this, since it implies the existence of an underlying system. It should inspire us to discover and exploit that system. We may take comfort, too, from the fact that small children use so much less vocabulary than we do — and then suddenly we realise that we have stumbled on part of their secret: children learn one stratum of vocabulary thoroughly, complete with noun genders, before proceeding to the next, and so on. This natural stratification undoubtedly serves them well when it comes to gender assignment, and we shall see why this is so.

As I have said, most students of French as a second language acquire vastly greater competence in handling verb forms than in assigning genders. There is in my experience a great divergence in the presentation of these aspects of French grammar on the part both of teachers and of manuals. Verbs are normally presented systematically. For example, the verbs *avoir* and *être* are presented early, as are *-er* verbs, to be followed by verbs in *-ir* and *-re*, as well as other irregular verbs. For gender, however, teachers and manuals tend to trust to nature. Occasionally, some rules are formulated, but they appear to be at least partially contradictory. Students soon realise that the rules are limited in some way, but for the most part their best efforts do not allow them to define the limitations. The majority finally come to the conclusion that the only solution is to learn the gender of each noun by rote, but are awed by the enormity of the task. Considering that speakers are known to use several thousand words, even for the simplest forms of communication, this is hardly surprising.

This book is based on the assumption that method can be applied to the acquisition of gender assignment patterns. We shall begin by examining the strategies which allow children to acquire genders with such apparent ease. We shall then look at the gender of different types of nouns, sub-dividing them as follows into categories which are related to gender assignment:

(1) Animate nouns: that is, nouns designating people or animals versus those designating objects or ideas (inanimate nouns). For the vast majority of nouns used for people, and a number of those for animals, the link between male and masculine gender, female and feminine gender, plays a major part.

(2) Simple inanimate nouns: words such as *porte, fleur, vertu*, in which only one meaningful element is recognisable. These are contrasted with complex nouns: those which contain more than one meaningful element, such as *organisation, pause-café, coupe-papier*.

(3) Complex inanimate nouns:
   (a) Nouns formed by the addition of a suffix, sometimes called derivates. Examples are *organisation* (organis- + -ation), *boulangerie* (boulang(er)- + -erie).
   (b) Compounds: those formed by a combination of meaningful elements other than word plus suffix. Examples are *pause-café, mine de sel, compte-gouttes*.

(4) Two types of nouns formed by shortening: lexical abbreviations (those in which part of the phonetic form of the noun is cut off), and acronyms (those in which initials are used instead of whole words). Examples are *photo* (*photographie*), *télé* (*télévision*), *sida* (*syndrome d'immuno-déficience acquise*), TGV (*train à grande vitesse*).

(5) Conglomerates: nouns formed from a phrase or sentence, such as *rendez-vous*.

(6) A special category of complex nouns: technical and 'learned' words which have their own rules of formation, and hence also of gender assignment, based on those of Greek or Latin. Although we use the term 'learned' for them because of their origins, many such nouns find their way into frequent usage. Examples are *téléphone*, *thermomètre*, *psychologie*, *claustrophobie*.

In addition to looking at the gender assignment patterns for all of these categories, we shall consider two special groups which have particular importance for gender assignment: that of inanimate nouns for which meaning appears to play a prominent part, and that of homophones (pairs and groups of nouns of identical form).

At the lowest (most frequent) level of vocabulary, you will probably find it necessary to do some conscious committing to memory, but there are tendencies associated with phonetic form which help to reduce such learning to a minimum. The more you progress, however, the more systematic gender assignment becomes, and the less conscious attention you should have to give it. As with verb forms, the most difficult part of the work occurs as you start to learn French.

Activities suggested at the end of each chapter are designed to heighten your awareness of gender and its functions in French, to encourage liberal use of gender markers for this purpose, and to help you to consolidate the knowledge you have at each level before proceeding to the next. They are designed to serve the needs of classes as well as those working alone. If you are studying independently, simply avoid the activities which require a group, but do try to find either a colleague to cooperate with you or a Francophone willing to converse with you.

Readers of this book will usually have acquired a considerable amount of French vocabulary already. Before going further, you may be interested to discover where you stand in the matter of using the correct gender. We therefore start with a test to help you evaluate your 'gender assignment competence'.

Testing Your Gender Assignment Competence

The following test will help you to determine how accurate you are in assigning gender correctly to some of the most frequent French words.

Test I

After each of the following words, insert **m** or **f** to indicate the gender.

Before entering the answers, you might want to photocopy the test. Then, you can try it again later and compare the scores.

lessive	( )	idée	( )	génie	( )
goutte	( )	affiche	( )	machine	( )
chemin	( )	luxe	( )	emploi	( )
repas	( )	trou	( )	vertu	( )
barbe	( )	ministère	( )	film	( )
école	( )	piège	( )	poème	( )
menace	( )	temps	( )	paix	( )
incendie	( )	banane	( )	milieu	( )
horloge	( )	queue	( )	ambulance	( )
étoffe	( )	cave	( )	boutique	( )
courage	( )	empire	( )	mois	( )
ligne	( )	faim	( )	chambre	( )
plage	( )	état	( )	fusil	( )
acier	( )	navire	( )	équipe	( )
heure	( )	soupe	( )	poivre	( )
marche	( )	coude	( )	poche	( )
feuille	( )	automobile	( )	brouillard	( )
nuit	( )	date	( )		

Now, check your answers against the correct ones, which are to be found on page 64. Note your score out of 50 and the date:

Score _____ Date _____

(Additional tests, based on the nouns used as examples in this book, are to be found on page 63)

If you have all answers correct, congratulations. If not, you are in good company. Many fluent speakers of French as a second language would hate to admit how often they use well-tried evasion strategies to hide their uncertainty about a gender. The fact remains that this is a serious problem which will not disappear of its own accord. You need to take action. The nouns used in this test occur frequently. The genders of such nouns are vitally important for two reasons. First, just because they are frequent: if you regularly use the wrong genders for words in this stratum of vocabulary, you will be making a very large number of errors. Worse, the genders of a large group of compounds are directly obtained from the simple noun which serves as the base (for instance, *drap* in *drap-housse*, which is therefore masculine like *drap*). As you can see, allowing yourself to be slipshod about the gender of frequent simple nouns is all too likely to create a snowball effect. In my opinion, we should aim at a perfect score for words in this category. That is what native speakers of French acquire very early.

You need to improve your gender mastery, not because it is catastrophic to produce the wrong gender from time to time, but rather because it is important, for reasons I will explain shortly, to accustom yourself to paying attention to gender markers, and to deriving information from them. When a student of French regularly makes gender errors, it is as if an athlete regularly stumbles in a trial run. It suggests that the training method needs to be modified or intensified. That is what we shall try to do for gender learning in the remainder of this book.

Learning from Children about Learning Genders

As has already been said, Francophone children learn at an early age to assign genders with uncanny accuracy. Surely it would be worth our while to look at some of the linguistic habits which enable them to do so?

It is well known that young children enjoy detailed description. They would rather hear about 'une belle grande voiture blanche' (a beautiful, big white car) than simply about 'une voiture blanche' (a white car). Research has shown that they will try to describe an object minutely rather than simply use an expression such as 'une des voitures'. And, of course, children tend to use the most frequent adjectives.

In French, it happens that some of the most frequent adjectives possess a characteristic which is important in relation to the learning of genders: the masculine and feminine forms are quite clearly distinguished. The following are some examples:

grand	grande
bon	bonne
petit	petite
beau	belle
laid	laide
mauvais	mauvaise
vieux	vieille
blanc	blanche
vert	verte
brun	brune
important	importante
dangereux	dangereuse
premier	première
dernier	dernière

Obviously, by using such adjectives, and using them in abundance, children put particular emphasis on gender distinctions. Anglophone students, on the other hand, tend to favour the opposite kind of adjectives: those which do not change according to the gender of the noun they modify. Some of their favourites are *énorme, magnifique, extraordinaire, terrible.* These are, of course, easy to use not only because they do not show gender, but also because they have similar form and meaning in English and French. In order to improve or perfect your mastery of gender, you should try, when possible, to select, or at least not avoid, the first kind.

Children also tend to favour the following types of structures:

Sentences containing a demonstrative pronoun (*celui-ci, celui-là, celle-ci, celle-là*):

Moi, je préfère celle-ci à celle-là.

Sentences with emphatic construction:

La maison, elle est belle et grande.
Je la veux, la banane.

An interrogative sentence requiring the repetition of the subject or the object:

Est-ce qu'elle est chaude, la soupe?
La pomme, est-ce qu'elle est bonne?
Tu la veux, l'orange?

All of these structures require the speaker to know with certainty which gender to assign to a noun they are using. For this reason, Anglophones often avoid them. Indeed, teachers sometimes advise students to ask questions by means of a simple change of intonation, or insertion of a question mark in writing (La soupe est chaude?). The advice is unwise both because it cramps the speaker's style and, more important from our point of view, because it enables the speaker in some cases to avoid the gender issue altogether, as in 'Tu trouves ces maisons terribles?'

Another advantage French-speaking children have in learning genders is that many of the nouns they use are amongst the most frequent. This helps them because the most frequent nouns are simple (as distinct from derived or compound), and we shall see that the three categories exhibit essential differences as regards gender assignment. Heavy use of the simple nouns helps them to establish the genders for that category firmly in their memory, and so to keep them largely separate from the other layers of vocabulary. Adults cannot reasonably be expected to copy them in this respect, but can compensate to a considerable extent by increasing their awareness of the different rules for gender assignment which affect various types of nouns.

Another prop which helps to entrench gender firmly in the memory of those growing up in a Francophone community is the use of fixed expressions in which gender is emphasised. Examples include the following, which are heard frequently in day-to-day greetings or under special circumstances:

bonjour
bonne nuit
bonne année
bonne fin de semaine
bon weekend
de belles vacances
une belle journée
un beau voyage
bonne chance
bonne fête

In this book, I propose to mimic the early experience of Francophones as far as possible by using as examples nouns selected from frequent vocabulary, by encouraging the use of adjectives marked for gender, and by favouring sentence structures which emphasise gender.

Activities

(1) If possible, listen in on a group of young Francophone children (perhaps a kindergarten or senior day-care would allow you to observe ordinary activities for an hour or two). Note the types of nouns, adjectives and structures the children use.

(2) Go through a passage of written French such as a magazine article, highlighting all the gender markers (adjectives, articles, pronouns etc. which indicate gender). Next, use a different coloured highlighter to mark all adjectives, articles and pronouns which do *not* indicate gender. Rewrite the passage, inserting as many gender markers as possible.

(3) Rewrite a composition of your own so that the genders are emphasised.

(4) Describe in detail a car, boat, item of sports equipment or other item that you own or would like to acquire. Make sure that anyone listening to or reading your description would be able to deduce the gender of every noun used.

(5) You need to find some extra money. Write an advertisement for radio describing some items you want to sell. Describe the items carefully, so as to attract buyers, using adjectives which mark gender.

The Great Divide: Semantic Versus Grammatical Gender

If we are to understand how gender functions in French, we must first separate the gender of animate nouns (in which there are definite reflections of 'real' gender) from that of inanimate nouns (which works primarily as a system for simply classifying nouns). That is to say that it groups words according to the way they behave in a sentence rather than telling us anything about their meaning. The first type is usually called 'semantic gender', the second 'grammatical gender'. Examples of the first type of gender, in which we see a clear link between sex and gender, are:

garçon, masculine, versus *fille*, feminine.

This pair may be compared to

pied, masculine, versus *main* feminine,

the last two being instances of grammatical gender. It is by no means easy to find many examples of words for human beings in which the sex–gender link is as uncomplicated as in the case of *garçon* and *fille*. Semantic gender was at one time called 'natural gender'. The term has fallen out of favour, no doubt because we have become more aware of the fact that there is much convention in the factors governing the gender of animate nouns, in French as well as in other Indo-European languages. The word *homme* ('man', 'mankind', and in the plural 'people') provides a good example.

There is, of course, considerable crossover between the two categories of gender in French, because they affect the structure of a sentence in the same way, and because even the gender of animate nouns does not consistently reflect reality. However, the distinction remains fundamental.

Semantic Gender: The Gender of Animate Nouns

Beginners are always amazed to discover that *personne* and *sentinelle* are feminine in French. After all, 'a person' can be a man, and until very recently 'a sentinel' was almost invariably a man, so why should a person and a sentinel not be designated by masculine

10

words? How, the beginner implies, can linguistic gender run counter to the way in which we normally represent the sexes?

In other words, we presuppose a certain relationship between the gender of words and the biological or sociological gender of the persons designated by those words. This is not surprising in view of the association between these two factors which is so well entrenched in many of the Indo-European languages most familiar to Anglophone learners. Those of us who know German, Italian, Spanish, or Latin, for example, have long since learned to associate masculine with male and feminine with female, at least at the human level.

The equation largely holds good for French as regards humans, and where the reference is to a single known person, as in

le médecin que j'ai consulté

l'infirmière qui m'a donné une injection.

However, the demands, at first of feminists, but later of most liberal-thinking people, for gender-neutral language have taught us to look more critically at assumptions concerning the use of the masculine as a singular or plural generic.

For animals, the conventions are only partially similar. The number of animal names following the masculine–male and feminine–female pattern is modest. The majority are designated by a single term which serves for both male and female. *Souris*, for instance is feminine, even if the individual animal being talked about is a male, or perhaps specifically credited with being a father, as in a children's story or a biological treatise. The same applies to *baleine*. *Moustique*, on the other hand, is masculine although the stinging variety of mosquito, to which we mostly refer in ordinary speech, is the female. The few feminine generics at the human level, like *personne* and *sentinelle*, are just examples of a similar phenomenon occurring at the human level, where one does not expect to find it.

We can sum the situation up by stating that, in the realm of animate words in general, linguistic gender in French is strongly influenced by 'real' gender, although there is no one-to-one relationship between them. (Note that you cannot generalise from one language to another on this point, even when they are quite closely related. French and German, for example, as most will know, show considerable differences.)

La sentinelle

Grammatical Gender: The Gender of Inanimates

For those who find it strange that the relationship between sex and gender is neither simple nor constant, the gender of inanimate words presents an apparently much more difficult dilemma. Why should we give *chaise, fleur* and *plante* the gender associated with the female, whereas *fauteuil, arbre* and *fruit* receive that which is usually given to males? We tend to look for a semantic reason for the gender assigned even to inanimate nouns, but attempting to do this will only add to the learner's frustrations. Linguists, grammarians and language learners have so far looked in vain for explanations of gender assignment in French based systematically on characteristics of the type of object denoted, such as size, shape, or the attitude of humans towards them. It is clear that, at least for the moment, we must look to factors other than meaning to explain the gender of the vast majority of words designating inanimates.

We shall deal with the two categories separately (except as regards homophones), starting with the gender of inanimates, which present by far the greater difficulty for Anglophone learners. The gender of animates will be addressed separately in a later chapter.

Activities

(1) Write a newspaper article protesting against (or defending) the practice of keeping wild animals in captivity.

(2) Tell or write a children's story (or an adults' story on the model of *Animal Farm*) in which animals act like human beings. Make your story consistent with the gender of the animals which appear as characters. (For example, *la souris* takes the role of a woman, *le cochon* that of a man.)

(3) Prepare a speech or write a newspaper article about sex stereotypes in the domain of fashion or in the working world as they affect a variety of types of people.

The Link Between Gender and Phonetic Word Ending

Most people who have any theories at all about how genders are assigned in French look to the influence of the phonetic ending of the word. For example, they may be aware of the fact that the consonant at the end of *voyage* suggests masculine gender. As we shall see, 94% of words ending in [ʒ] are indeed masculine. Other phonetic endings are mostly less powerful indicators of gender. As has already been said, this is not the only factor at work. We shall also see that the phonetic rules (those which relate the phonetic ending of a word to its gender) are far weaker than those which are based on the structure of the noun or those based on its meaning. In fact, the reader should be warned at the outset that the phonetic 'rules' should really be termed tendencies. The strongest of them applies to 100% of cases of the ending concerned. Others cover as few as just over 60%, and four endings provide no clue at all as to gender. It also happens that some of the words which run counter to the phonetic rules are amongst the most frequent. For example, *cage, plage* and *rage* are feminine, despite having a predominantly masculine ending, and they are, of course, amongst the words which both native speakers and learners of French as a second language would be likely to acquire early.

This section will show what help can be obtained in deciding how to assign gender from rules based on the phonetic endings of words, and present a set of examples to illustrate the rules. As in the natural language acquisition process, exceptions are also presented. One of the important facts we know about acquisition is that the mature native speaker knows not only which gender is associated with which ending, but also how widely applicable that rule is. An impressive and fascinating piece of research has shown that native speakers of French, faced with unknown words, will divide words with a given phonetic ending into masculine and feminine so as to produce in the sample the same proportion of 'exceptions' to the relevant phonetic rule as would apply to the language as a whole. The student of French as a second language who aims at near-native quality should ideally obtain this kind of knowledge in a natural manner, as well as knowing what the regular gender associated with an ending would be. Realistically, there is only one way to do this. It is to learn the genders of the most used words as thoroughly as does the young native speaker of French.

The phonetic rules we have apply to all types of French nouns: animate or inanimate and simple, derived or compound. Examples given here to illustrate the phonetic rules, however, are for the most part simple inanimate nouns, since these are the ones for which little other help is available in deciding the gender.

We can start by disposing of the category of endings which tell us nothing about gender. The endings which are 'neutral' in French are as follows:

[p] as in *type* m, *lampe* f
[t] as in *mythe* m, *date* f
[l] as in *bal* m, *balle* f
[e] as in *papier* m, *année* f

You will notice that the endings are represented by phonetic signs (those enclosed in square brackets). These are not easy for everyone to read, so examples are provided to show or remind the reader how they are pronounced. The consonants in the above list don't present any difficulty, but remember that only the closed [e] is neutral. Open [ɛ], as in *paquet, objet* favours the masculine.

The genders even of words with these neutral endings still do not all have to be learned simply by rote: there are amongst them blocks which can be identified as being governed by a non-phonetic rule. One of the most important things to be learned is that in deciding genders we are always dealing with a number of intersecting rules, and that, however complex the interplay may at times seem, it is not too difficult for the average ten-year-old Francophone to have mastered.

Turning now to the positive side of the phonetic rules, we start with the masculine endings, and then move on to the feminine. The endings are given in approximately descending order of usefulness. That is to say that those endings which are most consistently 'regular' in terms of gender are listed first. However, in the interests of simplicity I have grouped the masculine vowels together. In each category, a selection of frequent nouns provides 'correct' examples. Important exceptions are also listed, and the number of 'correct' and 'incorrect' examples reflect to some extent the proportions known to exist in the language as a whole. (However, I considered it important to include the extremely frequent counter-examples, so the correspondence between numbers of exceptions existing in the language and the number given here is far from precise.) Many of the words used are to be found in *le français fondamental*, which contains 3000 words considered to be amongst the most frequent in French, or in vocabulary lists designed for students at the intermediate level. Others are words much used in present-day French, chosen for their value both as vocabulary and as examples of the role of the phonetic ending in gender assignment.

A percentage is indicated after each phonetic ending showing the proportion of nouns with masculine gender for that ending. This information is derived from the work of Tucker, Rigault & Lambert (1970).

Note that feminine e, sometimes pronounced in liaison (as in *verre, village, tube, chose*), is not counted as a vowel ending.

Masculine Endings

The first of the following columns shows the phonetic ending for the group in question. The second indicates the proportion of masculines found in French as a whole for that ending. The third shows regular (masculine) examples, and the fourth irregular (feminine) examples with the same ending.

Phonetic ending	Per cent masc.	Masculine (regular)	Feminine (exceptions)
[œ̃]	100%	un parfum emprunt	(No feminine examples)
[ɛ̃]	99%	bain pain pin bouquin bassin	faim fin
[ã]	99%	banc camp champ	dent
[ø]	97%	peu pneu aveu jeu voeu	queue banlieue
[o]	97%	pot tricot	eau peau

		sabot	chaux
		dos	
		kilo	
		numéro	
		seau	
		couteau	
		micro	
[ɛ]	90%	paquet	haie
		fait	baie
		buffet	plaie
		billet	paix
		sommet	paie
		robinet	craie
		respect	
		arrêt	
		trait	
		portrait	
		souhait	
		objet	
[u]	88%	cou	boue
		coup	moue
		caillou	
		houx	
		verrou	
		bijou	
		chou	
[a]	83%	débat	polka
		mandat	foi
		camélia	villa
		foie	fois
		résultat	joie
		droit	croix
		matelas	proie
		choix	soie
		poids	
		bois	
		mois	
		tabac	
		plat	
		drap	
		contrat	

[y]	72%	début	vertu
		malentendu	tenue
		salut	avenue
		menu	rue
		tissu	statue
		reçu	vue
		jus	
		statut	
		abus	
		contenu	
		substitut	
[ʒ]	94%	âge	cage
		barrage	rage
		dommage	plage
		étage	image
		fromage	nage
		garage	neige
		linge	orange (meaning fruit)
		nuage	gorge
		ouvrage	horloge
		village	
		voyage	
		siège	
		ménage	
		langage	
[m]	92%	drame	flamme
		blâme	crème
		problème	rime
		poème	estime
		thème	gomme
		système	arme
		crime	rame
		régime	forme
		dôme	
		royaume	
		tome	
		terme	
		germe	
		anthème	
		rythme	
		légume	

[f]	89%	télégraphe	carafe
		rosbif	agrafe
		tarif	coiffe
		triomphe	soif
		paragraphe	étoffe
		grief	
		golfe	
		relief	
[r]	75%	bar	plupart
		fard	foire
		phare	armoire
		cigare	poire
		lard	victoire
		hectare	histoire
		genre	chambre
		équilibre	prière
		massacre	pierre
		air	mer
		sommaire	heure
		tonnerre	fleur
		verre	peur
		vers (verse)	saveur
		ver (worm)	rencontre
		désert	
		dessert	
		coeur	
		litre	
		beurre	
		poivre	
		givre	
[g]	73%	iceberg	bague
		catalogue	blague
		monologue	meringue
		prologue	
[k]	67%	cognac	flaque
		sac	époque
		parc	marque
		manque	
		bac	
		lac	
		bric-à-brac	

[b]	65%	globe	jambe
		tube	bombe
		cube	aube
		microbe	
		club	

Feminine Endings

The first of the following columns shows the phonetic ending for the group. The second indicates the proportion of feminines found in French for that ending. The third shows regular (feminine) examples, and the fourth irregular (masculine) examples with the same ending.

Phonetic ending	Percent fem.	Feminine (regular)	Masculine (exceptions)
[z]	90%	blouse	onze
		chose	douze
		crise	trapèze
		chemise	manganèse
		église	bronze
		excuse	vase (flower vase)
		fraise	
		framboise	
		phrase	
		rose	
		surprise	
		valise	
		vase (mud)	
[i]	83%	comédie	habit
		mélodie	ski
		mélancolie	midi
		agonie	profit
		manie	génie
		insomnie	
		pneumonie	
		poésie	
		ironie	
		hernie	
[ʃ]	70%	chanson	jambon
		boisson	flocon
		fonction	balcon

		leçon	wagon
		maison	crayon
		moisson	camion
		nation	savon
		pension	
		prison	
		rançon	
		cuisson	
		raison	
		saison	
[n]	69%	chaîne	chêne
		couronne	domaine
		corne	crâne
		douane	téléphone
		fortune	
		lune	
		mine	
		plaine	
		prune	
		semaine	
		veine	
[v]	69%	grève	fleuve
		olive	rêve
		preuve	
		rive	
		cave	
		fève	
		archives	
[j]	68%	aiguille	accueil
		bataille	conseil
		bouteille	outil
		famille	seuil
		feuille	soleil
		maille	
		oreille	
		taille	
		veille	
[ʃ]	66%	manche (sleeve)	manche (handle)
		cloche	reproche
		couche	dimanche
		fourche	

planche
ruche
tache
tâche
pêche
poche
quiche
recherche

[d]	62%		
		aide	coude
		bande	liquide
		concorde	monde
		corde	sud
		demande	
		étude	
		garde (guard duty)	
		méthode	
		période	
		viande	

[s]	62%		
		bourse	divorce
		brosse	édifice
		course	exercice
		cuisse	os
		chance	sexe
		chasse	silence
		dépense	
		expérience	
		force	
		justice	
		mousse (foam)	
		pièce	
		race	

[ɲ]	61%		
		besogne	peigne
		consigne	champagne (wine)
		montagne	règne
		vigne	
		beigne	
		ligne	

The lists of examples given for the phonetic rules have been designed to reinforce the knowledge that, although these rules offer a good starting point for your sorting of nouns by gender, they are no more than a guide.

There are two additional points worth noting in the context of the phonetic rules:

(1) We tend to assume that 50% of French nouns are masculine, as though the matter were decided by the laws of chance. This is not so. The research of Tucker, Rigault & Lambert (1970) has shown that the proportion of masculine nouns in French is in fact 61%. In the absence of other clues to the gender of a noun, therefore, it is prudent to bet on masculine. Also, in the light of this information, knowing that 61% of nouns ending in [ɲ] are feminine, as in the last category illustrated, is more useful information than might at first appear, since this actually amounts to a reversal of the proportions for the language as a whole.

(2) Some of the most important exceptions to the phonetic rules are governed by the rules based on noun structure, which will be explained in a later chapter. Others are covered by the semantic rules, to which we turn next. The value of both these sets of rules is precisely that, in French, they supply some of the considerable need left by the rather weak phonetic rules. Both the morphological and the semantic rules have the virtue of determining gender with near certainty.

You may well ask what is the point of setting out 'rules' for which there are so many exceptions. There are several reasons for doing so. The first is that most learners of French as a second language intuitively try to do this for themselves. Most of us, however, remember the disappointment of discovering that the system did not allow us to predict gender. In fact, recognising this is in itself a move in the right direction, since it should alert us to the existence of other sets of rules. It is by playing them one against the other that we eventually become skilled at sorting nouns according to their gender.

Summing Up

The information provided in this chapter can be summarised as follows:

Masculine vowel endings

All vowel endings are masculine except [e], as in *papier, année,* which is neutral, [i] as in *prairie,* and [ɔ̃] as in *maison.* The last two are predominantly feminine endings. Masculine and feminine endings, in descending order of value are as follows:

Masculine vowel endings

Over 90%   [æ̃], as in *un*
[ɑ̃], as in *plan*
[ɛ̃], as in *pain*
[ø], as in *peu*
[o], as in *pot*
[ɛ], as in *balai*

Over 80%   [u], as in *bout*
[a], as in *chocolat*

Over 70%   [y], as in *reçu*

Masculine consonant endings

Over 90%   [ʒ], as in *voyage*
[m], as in *gramme*

Over 80%   [f], as in *oeuf*

Over 70%   [r], as in *beurre*

Over 60%   [g], as in *catalogue*
[k], as in *bec*
[b], as in *tube*

Feminine vowel endings

Over 60%   [ɔ̃], as in *maison*
[i], as in *prairie*

Feminine consonant endings

90%   [z], as in *bise*

Over 60%   [n], as in *peine*
[v], as in *rive*
[j], as in *paille*
[ʃ], as in *tâche*
[d], as in *bande*
[s], as in *chance*
[ɲ], as in *ligne*

It would obviously be worthwhile to pay particular attention to the endings which can determine gender for a very high proportion of nouns.

If you are blessed with a good memory, you may want to memorise this information. It would certainly help you to make an educated guess when in doubt. These indications, however, are obviously too clumsy a tool to use as a general rule. There is no infallible solution for the simple words other than to learn the genders, giving particular attention to those which have the 'wrong' gender according to the phonetic rules. Remember, however, that you can learn the genders quickly, easily and above all *naturally* by always using the correct gender with a noun, and by choosing the types of adjectives and structures which emphasise gender.

Activities

(1) If you are working with a partner or a group, make a set of cards, each of which shows one of the words serving as examples in this chapter. Each person in turn picks three cards and delivers a speech (serious or funny) using the words picked. Try to mark the genders as clearly as possible.

(2) If you are working alone, write a text using as many as possible of the examples in this chapter. Try to mark the genders of the words clearly.

(3) Write a text, again using words found in this chapter, this time trying not to betray the gender of any noun in it. (This will show you how constrained you will be in French if you are unable to use genders freely.)

Meaning and the Gender of Inanimate Nouns

The gender of inanimate nouns seems in general to bear little or no relationship to the meaning of individual words. However, French includes a certain number of groups in which the constant association with one gender is quite striking. French grammars have traditionally referred to such cases, but the information provided by them has proved difficult to apply in practice, and often somewhat confusing from the theoretical point of view. In particular, one wonders why meaning should be linked to gender in only a small proportion of cases. Where and why, one wonders, should this criterion stop being applied?

In fact, if you look closely at the lists of nouns supposedly grouped by meaning associated with gender, you will see that they are amongst the most frequently used in the language, and form a cluster which young Francophones would undoubtedly acquire early.

A second, less obvious feature is that a number of the nouns grouped in this way have the opposite gender to that which they should have under the phonetic rules. Perhaps the grammarians stumbled intuitively on an important set of exceptions to these rules. In any case, the semantic rules can be useful in the process of acquiring gender mastery provided you realise that looking for semantic grouping of inanimate nouns is unlikely to be fruitful outside the limits of the lists given here.

Note also that, although derived and compound nouns are, as you would expect, few and far between amongst the most frequent words in French, these semantic groups include a considerable proportion.

The semantic groups for gender assignment are as follows.

Masculine Groups

(1) The days of the week, the months and the seasons:

   lundi, mardi, mercredi, jeudi, vendredi, samedi, dimanche

   janvier, février, mars, avril, mai, juin, juillet, août, septembre, octobre, novembre, décembre

   printemps, été, automne, hiver

26

Un hiver particulièrement froid

It is worth noting that all the names of days of the week conflict with the phonetic rules for gender which would apply to them. These words are not used with a great variety of adjectives. Their gender, however, is abundantly illustrated by expressions such as the following:

lundi prochain
samedi dernier
l'hiver suivant
Je ne travaille pas le dimanche
J'y vais tous les jeudis

(2) The points of the compass:

nord, sud, est, ouest, and the compounds *sud-est* etc.

Gender markers are frequently shown in expressions such as:

le vent du nord
J'habite au sud de Montréal

Note that *sud* has an ending normally associated with the feminine, and that of *est* and *ouest* is neutral as to gender.

(3) Names of languages:

le français, le roumain, le swahili

(4) Chemical elements and other metals. Some of those which occur most frequently are:

argent, fer, iode, hydrogène, oxygène, tungstène, manganèse, bronze

(5) Letters of the alphabet and cardinal numbers. Examples are:

un a mal formé
le quatorze juillet

(6) Metric measures:

gramme, litre, mètre, volt, watt, hectare and all compounds of these, such as *milligramme, centigramme, kilogramme*

Common examples showing gender are:

un litre de lait
un kilo de beurre
C'est à un bon kilomètre d'ici

Note the exceptions: *tonne, kilotonne, calorie, kilocalorie*, all feminine. But *calorie* is gradually being replaced by *joule* (m).

(7) Colours. Examples are:

le bleu
le rose
un orange éclatant
un aubergine doux

(*Orange* and *aubergine*, on the other hand, are feminine when they refer to the fruit or vegetable.)

(8 Wines and cheeses. Examples are:

le chèvre
le gruyère
le madère
le champagne

Again, we have cases in which a word is masculine if it means cheese or wine (as the case may be), but feminine in another meaning. Compare:

la Champagne (Champagne country)
la chèvre (the goat)

(9) Types of aircraft:

un DC9
un 747
un Lockheed

Note in particular *le Concorde* (the aircraft), but *la concorde* (concord, harmony).

(10) Trees. Examples are:

> chêne
> saule
> platane
> érable
> tilleul

and many names in *-ier*, such as

> bananier
> pommier
> poirier
> dattier

Note the three exceptions:

> *yeuse, épinette, sapinette*, all feminine.

Feminine groups

(1) Feast days:

> *la Saint-Jean Baptiste*
> *la Toussaint*
> *les Pâques fleuries* (Palm Sunday)

Note that *Pâques* and *Noël* both vary in gender. It is customary to say '*Joyeux Noël*', *but you may also hear people say 'à la prochaine Noël'*. On the other hand, one says '*Joyeuses Pâques*', but we write '*Pâques est célébré cette année le ...*'

(2 Academic disciplines:

> astronomie
> chimie
> linguistique
> physique
> théologie

Exceptions are *art, droit*, and the names of languages used in this sense: '*Nous étudions le français*'.

(3) Types of car:

> une deux chevaux
> une Ford
> une Peugeot
> une traction avant

Masculine exceptions are *sedan, break, coupé*. It should also be noted that in Québec the masculine is generally accepted for types of cars.

One of the semantic groups is particularly interesting and useful in that it leads us to a series of three groups with consistent gender relationships. A tree name in -*ier*, which as we have seen is masculine, in several cases becomes a feminine fruit name when the suffix -*ier* is dropped. (The written form also generally has an e added.) In some instances, you can also add a different suffix to the fruit name, giving a feminine word with the meaning 'plantation' or 'group of trees' as in the following series:

amande	amandier	amandaie
banane	bananier	bananeraie
cerise	cerisier	cerisaie
châtaigne	châtaignier	châtaigneraie
datte	dattier	
figue	figuier	
grenade	grenadier	
mangue	manguier	
orange	oranger	orangeraie
pamplemousse	pamplemoussier	
pêche	pêcher	
pin		pineraie
poire	poirier	
pomme	pommier	pommeraie
prune	prunier	
	sapin	sapinière

Note the exceptional cases in which the name of the fruit is masculine:

abricot m	*abricotier*
citron m	*citronnier*

It also seems that a majority of fruits are feminine. You might want to note a small number of other masculine exceptions:

bleuet ('blueberry', used in Canada, while *myrtille* is normal in France)
brugnon ('nectarine')
melon
raisin

As we have seen, the semantic groups include a majority of words which would be acquired early in life. They are also the type of words which would tend to occur in sequences of sentences providing similar contexts, so that the common gender element would be brought to the attention of those using them. It is easy to imagine, especially in children's conversations, series of sentences which refer to different trees, cars, colours and so on. Examples might run as follows:

> Notre voiture est plus grande que la vôtre.
> Mais la nôtre est une traction avant.
> Celle de mon père est une BMW.

> Ma couleur favorite est le bleu.
> La mienne est le rose.
> Je préfère le noir.

> J'aimerais planter un pommier ici.
> Moi, je préfère les poires aux pommes. Donc, j'aimerais mieux que ce soit un poirier.
> On pourrait très bien mettre un pommier, un poirier et un cerisier, puisque tout le monde aime les cerises!

Patterns of this kind would help the child speaker to acquire unerring accuracy in the assignment of gender to these words, many of which, as has been said, run counter to the phonetic rules. They would also help to reinforce awareness of the first morphological rules (those reflecting noun structure) which begin at this point to play their part.

We now follow the path of natural language acquisition by moving on to the morphological rules. You will have noticed that the semantic rules, although they apply to a relatively modest number of words, apply with only a small number of exceptions. The morphological rules are even stronger, as well as applying to a vastly larger, in theory almost infinite, number of words. We are therefore continuing our progression towards greater regularity in gender assignment.

Activities

(1) List the activities which fall regularly for you or members of your family on particular days of the week. Describe the problems which arise, for example, when three people need one car at the same time, or when everyone needs dinner at a different time.

(2) Invent three colours of the season (for clothing or cars), using nouns. (Examples: *sable, ciel.*) Indicate possible positive and negative associations of the words used which might affect the market reaction. For instance, would *ciel* have positive associa-

tions because it is worn by United Nations peacekeepers? What term could be used for peach colour to persuade working women to wear it?

(3) Describe in detail, using the names of individual types of trees, a reforestation project in an area you know. How was the previous forest destroyed? How can the new one be protected?

(4) Write a magazine or newspaper article on the impact of recent dietary theories which have affected eating and buying habits as regards meat, fruits, and cheese. Show the effects on trade and industry in your region.

The Role of Word Structure in Determining Gender

French, like all other languages, possesses rules which allow new words to be created from elements already existing in the language. These, which form an integral part of the linguistic system, are what we call 'morphological rules'. In the case of French, they include a formula which determines the gender of the new creation. The formula may apply directly (a word formed in such and such a manner will have a predetermined gender) or indirectly (for example, the word will assume the gender of one of the elements — a specified element — used in its formation). For instance, *brosse à dents* is feminine because *brosse* is feminine. A high proportion of less frequent words in French are formed in such a way, and the genders of the vast majority of them are, if you understand the model followed, completely or highly predictable. There is, however, an essential prerequisite for predicting the genders of a large number of them: you must have mastered the genders of simple nouns, since these constitute the base for many compound nouns, and the compounds based on nouns assume the genders of their base. You will have to learn the gender of a word such as *cuiller à soupe* if you do not know the gender of *cuiller*. Since this is a highly productive method of creating words, you can see how neglecting gender in the early stage of learning French can become to a considerable extent a self-perpetuating problem.

The following sets of examples represent the principal methods for creating nouns in French, as well as determining their gender. We start, following as usual the pattern of normal language acquisition by native speakers, with ordinary popular vocabulary, as distinct from the learned variety. (The latter is based on the classical languages, and is governed, as we shall see, by its own set of rules.)

In describing the methods of formation, I have followed the linguists' convention of assuming that the speaker creates the word each time a regular method of word-formation is used. These are models for using the resources of the French language to recreate words you have already met, to build words which you have not encountered although they do exist, or indeed to build words which do not yet exist. I do not mean to imply that you will necessarily invent many new words using these formulae. There is, however, no reason why a competent speaker or writer should not build words which did not previously exist. We do this without conscious effort in our own language.

Nouns Formed by Suffix

To form a noun by suffix, the speaker adds a meaningful element (suffix) at the end of an existing word. The suffixes are not able to function independently, but modify the word which constitutes the basis of the new form, often changing its grammatical category. Hence, an adjective becomes a noun (*national, nationalité*), or a verb becomes a noun, the usual ending of the verb being dropped (*exécuter, exécution*). In some cases in which a new noun is formed from an existing noun, the role of the suffix is to change the meaning of the original noun, as in *pomme, pommier; camion, camionnette*. Sometimes, the form of the base changes when the suffix is added, as in *libre, liberté*, or a consonant appears before the suffix, as in *polie, politesse*.

Forming a French noun by using a suffix allows you to assign the gender with certainty. The following lists provide examples of words produced by using the most prominent and productive types of suffixes serving to create nouns. It is not suggested that you learn the formulae. The object is to sensitise you to the existence of such a system, and to alert you to the mechanisms which govern it. Mastering the genders of words of this kind will follow almost automatically.

Note that we are still looking at the end of the noun for a clue as to its gender. However, the critical factor in these cases is not the phonetic ending but the suffix itself. If you compare the genders of the nouns formed by suffix with those that the *phonetic* ending would suggest in each case, there are two radical differences. First, the gender is not necessarily that which predominates for the phonetic ending, although there may be a large number of nouns formed by the suffix. (It follows, of course, that a given suffix may be responsible for a considerable proportion of the exceptions to the relevant phonetic rule.) Second, the rule based on the suffix applies virtually without exception, and therefore outweighs the phonetic rule. These rules also allow us to determine with certainty the gender of considerable groups of nouns with 'gender-neutral' phonetic endings.

Types of Nouns formed by Suffixation

(1) Verb + -*ation, -ition, -ution, -tion/-ssion* → feminine noun

admirer, admiration
exécuter, exécution
supposer, supposition
traduire, traduction
permettre, permission

(2) Adjective + -*té, -ité* → feminine noun

beau, beauté
égal,égalité
libre,liberté
national, nationalité
sain, santé

(3) Adjective or participle + -*ance, -ence* → feminine noun

abondant, abondance
absent, absence
différent, différence
naissant, naissance
préférant, préférence

(4) Cardinal number + -*ième* → masculine noun designating the appropriate fraction such as 'a fifth'

cinq, cinquième
six, sixième
sept, septième
huit, huitième

(5) Verb + -*ment* → masculine noun

changer, changement
enterrer, enterrement
régler, règlement
vêtir, vêtement

(6) Verb + -*age*, noun + -*age* → masculine noun

allier, alliage
apprentis, apprentissage
barrer, barrage
pâture, pâturage
pot, potage

(7) Noun + -*erie*, -*ie*, verb + -*erie* → feminine noun

>   boulanger, boulangerie
>   charcutier, charcuterie
>   libraire, librairie
>   maire, mairie
>   parfum, parfumerie

(8) Past participle + -*e* (feminine or 'mute' e) → feminine noun

>   allé, allée
>   craint, crainte
>   entrepris, entreprise
>   pensé, pensée
>   sorti, sortie

(9) Verb (stem or past participle) + -*ure* → feminine noun

>   aller, allure
>   ceint, ceinture
>   coiffer, coiffure
>   ouvert, ouverture
>   peint, peinture

(10) Feminine form of adjective + -*eur* → feminine noun

>   blanche, blancheur
>   grande, grandeur
>   horrible, horreur
>   profonde, profondeur
>   terrible, terreur

(11) Noun + -*er*, -*ier* → masculine noun = 'tree bearing' [base noun]

>   cerise, cerisier
>   citron, citronnier
>   poire, poirier
>   pomme, pommier

(12) Feminine form of adjective + -*esse* → feminine noun

>   délicate, délicatesse
>   polie, politesse
>   triste, tristesse
>   vieille, vieillesse

(13) Noun + -*ette* → feminine noun, usually with diminutive meaning

>   brique, briquette
>   camion, camionnette

char, charrette
cigare, cigarette

(14) Verb stem + -*sion* → feminine noun

conclure, conclusion
décider, décision
diviser, division

(15) Noun denoting number + -*aine* → feminine noun usually meaning an approximate quantity

six, sixaine 'six or so'
douze, douzaine 'a dozen'
vingt, vingtaine 'a score'

(16) Verb stem + -*oir* → masculine noun, which may denote an instrument performing the action expressed by the verb

arroser, arrosoir
compter, comptoir
raser, rasoir

(17 Noun + -*on* → masculine noun, sometimes with diminutive meaning

balle, ballon
carte, carton
veste, veston

(18) Noun + -*ée* → feminine noun = 'the duration or content of [base noun]'

an, année
jour, journée
matin, matinée
poing, poignée

Compound Nouns

We turn now to the compound nouns, those formed from the combination of meaningful elements other than base plus suffix. Compounds are sub-divided into two categories: verb-based and noun-based. (The 'learned' nouns are again omitted at this point.) There is a large and ever-growing number of compounds, the gender of which tends to create serious problems for the language learner. Native speakers, who mostly acquire them rather later than the simple and suffixed nouns, seem to have no difficulty in realising that the gender of the compounds does not, in many instances, depend at all on the ending, but rather on the morphological structure pure and simple. Anglophone learners, on the other hand, especially those who are linguistically mature, tend to acquire many of these words early in the process of learning the language because a high proportion of them share common roots with English words, so that they can readily be transferred with a little adaptation. In this way, the natural stratification which helps the native speaker is lost.

The remedy is obvious: you should train yourself to understand the formation of French words, and to identify the compounds as a special group in which the ending is unimportant as regards gender assignment.

Verb-based Compounds

We start with a group of compounds which, once you have decided to ignore the ending, is the easiest of all lexical groups in French from the gender point of view. The verb-based compounds are formed from a verb stem followed by a noun. The meaning is approximately 'that which [verb] [noun]'. So the literal meaning of *tire-bouchon* is 'that which pulls a cork' or 'an instrument for pulling corks'. Words formed in this way which designate an inanimate are overwhelmingly masculine. Other examples are:

> *aide-mémoire* 'that which helps your memory' (There is no word
> for this in English except the French one, which has been
> borrowed for this reason.)
> *allume-gaz* 'gas-lighter'
> *brise-vent* 'wind-break'
> *lave-vaisselle* 'dishwasher'
> *protège-dents* 'mouthguard', literally 'tooth-guard'

Exceptions to this rule are exceedingly rare. They include two botanical names: *perce-pierre* and *perce-muraille*. Other apparent exceptions usually designate people.

Noun-based Compounds

The rules governing the gender of noun-based compounds are less direct, but essentially easy for anyone who has mastered the gender of simple nouns. In these formations, a noun is modified by another noun, as in *jeu-concours*, or by a prepositional phrase (a phrase consisting of preposition and noun), as in *parking de dissuasion*. The noun which is to be modified serves as the base and gives its gender to the compound.

La pause-café

Noun plus noun compounds:

avion-citerne, 'air tanker', masculine like *avion*
drap-housse, 'duvet cover', masculine like *drap*
fiche-renvoi, 'reply coupon', feminine like *fiche*
pause-café, 'coffee break', feminine like *pause*

Noun plus prepositional phrase compounds:

cuiller à soupe 'soup spoon', feminine like *cuiller*
camion à remorque 'tow truck', masculine like *camion*
mine de sel 'salt-mine', feminine like *mine*

Some of this type do not display the preposition required to make sense of the compound:

station-service, 'service station', feminine like *station*
bas-nylon, 'nylon stockings', masculine like *bas*.

You will already have noticed that the element determining gender, far from being at the end of the word, is on the left-hand side of the compound. All you need in order to determine the gender of the noun-based compound is to know the gender of the first element.

Simple Conversion

Another major source of new nouns is simple grammatical conversion: a part of speech other than a noun is used as a noun without any modification. This process is so common that in many cases it passes almost unnoticed. Dictionaries often ignore it, as though it were part of the paradigm of the original word (the range of possible forms the word may assume), as indeed it is.

One very simple rule governs the gender of the majority of these creations: nouns designating inanimates and obtained from another part of speech without modification are usually masculine. This applies without exception to sentences or to parts of sentences containing more than one word.

Adjectives

The following nouns have the sense 'the colour x':

le rouge, le noir, un orange (criard).

Another series means 'the essential quality of being x':

l'absolu 'the absolute'
le chaud 'warmth'
le froid 'cold'
le liquide 'liquidity'
le vide 'empty space'

In other cases, an adjective assumes the meaning of an item which characteristically possesses the quality denoted by the adjective:

un blanc 'white wine'
le haut 'the top'
le double 'an object which is like another'
un bleu 'a bruise'

In the following sentences, an adjective functioning as a noun assumes the sense 'that which is [adjective]':

Il paraît que les garçons de six ans trouvent plus difficile que les filles du même âge tout ce qui relève du *linguistique*.
(It seems that boys of six find linguistic matters more difficult than do girls of the same age.)

Les *antidépresseurs* sont efficaces contre certaines dépressions d'origine biologique.
(Antidepressants are effective against certain types of depression of biological origin.)

Les *polluants* que nous craignons le plus sont ceux que nous ne voyons pas.
(The pollutants we fear the most are those we cannot see.)

In just a handful of cases, an adjective may become feminine because of regular association with a feminine noun. Frequent examples are:

la radiale 'arterial road'
la ronde 'circular space or dance, visit'
la moyenne 'median quantity or mark'
une droite, parallèle, perpendiculaire, verticale 'straight, parallel, perpendicular or vertical line'
une canine, incisive, molaire 'canine', 'incisor', or 'molar'

Verbs

The infinitive of a verb functions as a noun in the following examples:

Le coucher du soleil
Le dîner aura lieu à sept heures du soir.
Le manger et le boire sont parmi les plus grands plaisirs des humains.

Prepositions

Le pour et le contre
Prendre le dessus

Conglomerates

This is the term used for a whole sentence, or part of a sentence containing more than one word, when they serve as a noun.

un rendez-vous
un petit je ne sais quoi
un va-et-vient

Abbreviations

In present-day French, we often see nouns used so regularly in a shortened form that this has become the normal word. The gender remains that of the original noun (in some instances, a rather long compound). There are two types: lexical abbreviations and acronyms.

Lexical abbreviations

une photo, feminine like *photographie*
la manif, feminine like *manifestation*
la radio, feminine like *radiophonie*
la radio, feminine like *radiographie*
la fac, feminine like *faculté*
la télé, feminine like *télévision*
un vélo, masculine like *vélocipède*

le micro, masculine like *microphone*
le métro, masculine like *métropolitain*
le Bac, masculine like *Baccalauréat*

Acronyms (abbreviations by initialisation)

le PQ, masculine like *Parti Québécois*
le BQ, masculine like *Bloc Québécois*
le cégep, masculine like *collège d'éducation générale et pratique*
le DEUG, masculine like *Diplome d'études universitaires générales*
le sida, masculine like *syndrome d'immuno-déficience acquise ('AIDS')*
le TGV, masculine like *train grande vitesse*
la TVA, feminine like *taxe valeur ajoutée*
l'URSS, feminine like *Union des républiques socialistes soviétiques*
l'ONU, feminine like *Organisation des nations unies*

It is worth emphasising, obvious though the point is, that the ending of the abbreviated form is not directly relevant to its gender. New abbreviations are being created constantly, and many of them are amongst the nouns which do not conform to the phonetic rules for gender assignment.

You will have noticed that some, although not all, of the words abbreviated are in the 'learned' category, in that they denote academic or technological referents and they are based on words or morphemes directly derived from the classical languages. This is a category of nouns to which gender is assigned by special rules, and to which we now turn.

Technical and 'Learned' Nouns

Complex words based on Latin or Greek methods of word formation have provided, and continue to provide, a high proportion of technical and scientific vocabulary. Inevitably, many of them have entered ordinary usage, as the inventions they denote have become part of everyday life.

The following groups of nouns are masculine:

(1) Nouns designating units of measure based on *gramme*, which assume the gender of *gramme* itself:

centigramme, milligramme, kilogramme

(2) Words in *-gramme* designating a recording or representation of something:

télégramme, diagramme

(3) Words based on -*drome*:
   hippodrome, aérodrome, vélodrome
(4) Words based on -*cide*:
   herbicide, insecticide, spermicide, raticide
(5) Words based on -*mètre*:
   thermomètre, anémomètre, altimètre
(6) Words based on -*scope*:
   microscope, télescope, périscope
(7) Words for philosophical attitudes or political affiliations in -*isme*:
   athéisme, communisme, futurisme
(8) Words for instruments dealing with sounds:
   mégaphone, microphone, téléphone
   The following are feminine:
(1) Names of chemical substances ending in -*ine*:
   caféine, morphine, quinine, pénicilline
(2) Names of academic disciplines based on -*logie*:
   biologie, cardiologie, psychologie, sexologie
(3) Names of phobias or hearty dislikes in -*phobie*:
   agoraphobie, anglophobie, claustrophobie
(4) Terms for therapeutic treatments in -*thérapie*:
   hydrothérapie, psychothérapie, physiothérapie
(5) Names for types of knowledge in -*nomie*:
   agronomie, gastronomie, taxonomie
(6) Names of inflammations in -*ite*:
   appendicite, cystite, hépatite

Notice that in these groups of words the constant element which determines the gender is again on the right-hand side, at the end of the compound.

The technical or academic nature of the word as well as its Greek or Latin characteristics will alert you to the fact that you are dealing with a 'learned' noun. This knowledge will suggest that the last element will probably lead you to a model for the gender.

One feature of learned words is particularly worth noting. Many people regard the presence of -*e* at the end of a noun as an indication that it is probably feminine, and indeed it does provide a clue, in the absence of any stronger indication. As you may have noticed, however, most 'learned' nouns have -e at the end, and a good proportion of them are masculine. This clue must be discounted entirely for the 'learned' words.

Summing Up

To sum up the morphological rules, the structure of the noun determines the gender of the word. If you understand the relationship of your noun to other elements in French, the gender will usually be obvious to you. Realising that the number of derived and compound nouns in French is huge and constantly growing, we can be thankful for the fact that their genders are in most cases easily predictable. On the other hand, you will readily appreciate the need to assimilate the rules for them rather than either committing the genders to memory or hoping that the problem will take care of itself.

Activities

(1) Work with a partner. The first person makes a remark containing a verb other than *avoir*, *être*, and other extremely common ones. The second person replies, using a noun derived from the verb in the first sentence, as in the following example:

(i) J'admire ta coiffure.

(ii) Etant donné que tu détestes les permanentes, cette admiration ne me paraît pas sincère.

Other pairs of words you might use in this way are:

atterrir	atterrissage
changer	changement
conclure	conclusion
décider	décision
diviser	division
organiser	organisation
polluer	pollution
purifier	purification

Working alone or with a partner, you can apply the same method to a composition of your own, or to an existing passage in a newspaper or magazine. Once you have acquired the trick, you can use it in conversation with any reasonably fluent speaker. It will enrich your writing and conversation skills while teaching you a lot about gender.

(2) Search a magazine issue for derived or compound words which you did not already know. (Obviously, you should look for articles in which they are likely to be prominent, such as those on computers or popular entertainment.) Highlight the gender markers in the text. Where there are none, rewrite the sentence (or surrounding sentences) so as to indicate the gender.

(3) Invent new words on the models given in this chapter and use them in a speech or a written text. Challenge your partner or opposing team to find the 'imposters'. Examples might be *débouche-tuyaux, dépaternalisation, planche-à-glace* (for an ice-windsurfer), *sidatisation.*

(4) Describe a new device you have invented to help with kitchen chores. What kind of object is it? What size is it? What does it do? Your partner or opposing team is to create a new word for the invention on the model of *tire-bouchon*. Your aim can be serious or jocular. Examples could include *coupe-pain, essuie-vaisselle, lave-bouteilles, vide-poubelle,* or even *amuse-bébé.*

Biological or Sociological Gender: The Gender of Animate Nouns

It has already been said that the gender of animate nouns in French shows an association between male and masculine, female and feminine. However, this association is neither simple nor constant. In order to examine it more closely, I propose to separate the animates into two categories: human and non-human.

Words Designating Humans

A noun used in the singular to designate a human being of known sex will have masculine gender if the person is male and feminine if she is female, as in:

un garçon	une fille
un cuisinier	une cuisinière
un homme	une femme

It is, however, extremely difficult to find examples of nouns in which the male-masculine, female-feminine association is both simple and constant. In the plural, *garçon* is one of very few masculine nouns which still unambiguously imply maleness. There is no real possibility that *les garçons* will be a mixed group. *Les cuisiniers* and *les hommes*, however, may be of mixed or unknown sex unless this interpretation is excluded by the context. *Les cuisinières* and *les femmes*, on the other hand, do not admit of the possibility that men might form part of the group. On the whole, this is typical of the behaviour of nouns denoting humans in French, although there is a small number of feminine generic terms to which we shall return.

Almost any masculine animate noun is supposed, according to traditional grammar, to be capable of functioning as a generic. Hence, if a woman practises a profession traditionally dominated by men, she will, still according to traditional grammar, usually be designated by a masculine noun such as *un professeur, un médecin, un ingénieur*. Even in the case of a compound formed with *femme* following the professional title, the gender remains masculine (*un professeur-femme* etc.). In order to reestablish the female–feminine relationship, we have to turn the compound around, producing *une femme-médecin.* (The meaning is not quite the same, but many nevertheless prefer it.)

Today, writers responding to the complaints of feminists against the time-hallowed tradition, as well as the demands of governments, are producing an increasing number of feminine words for use as women's titles. This feminisation is achieved by different methods, as follows:

(1) The formation of a non-traditional feminine using an established method, but applying it to words which have not normally before been feminised:

   une professeure, une écrivaine

(2) A change of gender expressed simply by the feminisation of the article:

   une juge, une linguiste

(3) The formation of a feminine with *femme* as the first element, that which determines the gender:

   une femme-médecin, une femme-professeur

Conventionally correct sentences such as the following are increasingly unacceptable as societies become aware of the ambiguity of masculine nouns, especially those which have customarily carried heavy connotations concerning male dominance:

   Il faut l'intelligence d'un homme pour exploiter un ordinateur.

These days, you would be much more likely to insert an alternative feminine, as in the following:

   Il faut l'intelligence d'un homme ou d'une femme pour exploiter un ordinateur.

In a word, we might say that the association between linguistic and sociological or biological gender is currently being strengthened at the human level. The few feminine generics of relatively high frequency, on the other hand, have apparently retained their semantically neutral status. They are:

   personne, victime, recrue, sentinelle.

(Although in the past *recrue* and *sentinelle* denoted only men, since only men were admissible as soldiers, and are often quoted as examples of reverse sex–gender association, this is clearly no longer the case.)

Nouns Designating Non-human Animates

Nouns designating non-human animates (animals in the broadest sense) are variable as to the relationship between 'natural' and linguistic gender. You will, however, notice that the sex–gender association is strongest in the case of the animals which have the highest status in human eyes. The more important an animal is to us, the more likely we are to have an expression each for male and female, and to use a separate term for the generic, in which case the gender of the generic is masculine. So it is in the following categories:

boeuf:	taureau, vache
chat:	matou, chatte
cheval:	étalon, jument
daim:	cerf, biche
mouton:	bélier, brebis
porc:	verrat, truie

In another group, in which animals important to us appear, one of two terms designating respectively male and female is used as a generic. In this group, the masculine predominates, but the feminine serves as generic in three cases:

âne:	âne, ânesse
chien:	chien, chienne
lapin:	lapin, lapine
lion:	lion, lionne
loup:	loup, louve
pigeon:	pigeon, pigeonne
rat:	rat, rate
renard:	renard, renarde
tigre:	tigre, tigresse
abeille (f):	bourdon, abeille
chèvre (f):	bouc, chèvre
poule (f):	coq, poule

For the majority of animals, French possesses a single term, masculine or feminine, which is used for male and female, and also serves as the generic. The following examples include many of the commonest animal names:

(1) Mammals

(a) masculines

babouin, blaireau, caribou, castor, dauphin, gorille, hamster, kangourou, léopard, panda, phoque, raton laveur, rhinocéros, sanglier, zèbre

(b) feminines

antilope, baleine, belette, gazelle, girafe, hermine, hyène, panthère, souris, taupe

(2) Birds

(a) masculines

aigle, colin, corbeau, cygne, épervier, faucon, geai, merle, ortolan, vautour

(b) feminines

autruche, caille, chouette, cigogne, corneille, grive, grue, hirondelle, perdrix, tourtererelle

(3) Fish

(a) masculines

anchois, barbeau, exocet, hareng, maquereau, saumon, thon, turbot

(b) feminines

anguille, barbue, carpe, limande, merluche, morue, perche, sardine, sole, truite

(4) Insects

(a) masculines

amiral, carabe, criquet, frelon, grillon, hanneton, moucheron, moustique, papillon, perce-oreilles, taon, termite

(b) feminines

abeille, arpenteuse, cigale, coccinelle, fourmi, guêpe, mouche, puce, punaise, sauterelle

(5) Reptiles, amphibians, and other invertebrates

(a) masculines

crabe, crapaud, lézard, mille-pattes, serpent, ver

(b) feminines

couleuvre, grenouille, langouste, salamandre, tortue

(6) Molluscs

(a) masculines

casque, escargot, ormeau, pétoncle, strombe, triton

(b) feminines

coquille, crevette, huître, limace, palourde, porcelaine, vénus, grenouille, langouste, salamandre, tortue

It has already been said that the link between sex and gender is less important in the world of animals than in that of humans. On the surface, and at the level of individual nouns, the genders of animal names do not appear to reflect any particular characteristic of the animals represented. Overall, however, they present an interesting pattern which is not apparent in the above lists. A recent study has shown that the proportion of masculines in a representative corpus of animal names was as follows:

mammals	83.43%
birds	67.34%
fish	57.14%
insects	59.72%
molluscs	39.47%

One can almost say that the higher an animal is on the phylogenetic ladder, the more likely it is to be masculine. In the case of molluscs, the proportion of masculines is rather smaller than you would find in the French lexicon as a whole. One need not, of course, necessarily accept the view that mammals are superior animals, but one cannot deny that they are represented as such. These data certainly add grist to the mill of those who claim that the masculine cannot function at the human level as a neutral gender.

To sum up, what do you need to do to master the gender of animate nouns?

(1) Consider your position on gender-neutral language. If you are in favour of feminising titles and avoiding the so-called generic masculine, you will have to re-formulate many of the rules for agreement and reference given in traditional grammars and textbooks.

(2) Memorise the gender of the four relatively frequent feminine generics, and learn to use them with ease. They are:

personne, victime, sentinelle, recrue.

Of these, *personne* is by far the most important.

(3) Memorise the gender of the frequent animal names given here. Pay particular attention to the feminine gender of nouns designating large mammals, which many people find somewhat incongruous:

baleine, girafe, panthère

and to the following masculines denoting small creatures which are the subject of frequent errors:

crabe, moustique, termite.

La girafe et la panthère

Activities

(1) You are a journalist reporting on a serious accident involving a truck and a series of cars. Using the terms *personne* and *victime*, describe the state of some of the survivors and report the comments of some of the drivers. Alternatively, using the same words, report the opinions of several informants on air safety and airport security.

(2) Describe the fauna in your neighbourhood or an area in which you have spent a holiday. Indicate why you believe certain animals favour this region, and why others do not. Or indicate the principal environmental factors threatening particular species in your area.

(3) Using a number of examples, describe and comment on various manifestations of anthropomorphism in our culture, such as you might find in children's literature or television programmes. You might examine Winnie-the-Pooh or Barney the dinosaur as models for sex stereotyping, or analyse the role of the family in the Babar books.

Gender Makes the Difference:
Distinguishing Between Homophones

Homophones (words which sound the same) present special problems for those learning French, and we therefore need to give them special attention. Beginners naturally find themselves bewildered by pairs of words such as *le cours, la cour; le parti, la partie; le tour, la tour; le voile, la voile*. Gender sometimes plays a crucial part in distinguishing between such pairs.

At some point, probably quite early in the learning process, we become convinced that the phonetic structure of a word has an influence on its gender, and the theory is, as we have seen, partially correct. Beginners find homophones frustrating for two reasons: they probably find the homophones difficult to differentiate, and these awkward words sow confusion in their minds just when they thought they were starting to make sense of gender since, although the word they are considering is identical in form to another, the two have opposite genders. It seems that their theory is destroyed. Also, homophones are by no means uncommon. Some of them are amongst the very commonest words in French. As we shall discover, however, the world of homophones is less chaotic than it might appear at first sight.

Two types of homophones distinguished by gender exist in French. The first type consists of those which by some accident of history happen to have the same form as another word. We shall call these 'accidental homophones'. The second type, 'systematic homophones', consists of those which are created according to an established method: those which belong, as it were, to the paradigm of a word family. We shall look first at the accidental variety and then at the systematic. In order to assimilate the gender of accidental homophones, we can make use, as no doubt Francophone children do, of fixed or typical expressions using one or other of the group or pair. The systematic ones, once one has become aware of them, present no problem.

Note that in this chapter both animate and inanimate nouns are included.

Accidental Homophones

The following is a list of some of the most common accidental homophones distinguished by gender. In a few cases, such as that of *foi, foie* and *fois*, there is more than one homophone for one or other of the genders. Although gender is an important factor in distinguishing between words which sound identical, it is, of course, by no means the only one.

auteur m	hauteur f	
bal m	balle f	
boue f	bout m	
chaîne f	chêne m	
cour f	cours m	
crêpe m	crêpe f	
coq m	coque f	
eau f	haut m	
fois f	foi f	foie m
gaz m	gaze f	
mère f	maire m	
mal m	malle f	
manche m	manche f	
moule m	moule f	
mousse m	mousse f	
mur m	mûre f	
paire f	père m	
parti m	partie f	
peau f	pot m	
poêle m	poêle f	
sel m	selle f	
roux m	roue f	
somme m	somme f	
statue f	statut m	
tour m	tour f	
vase m	vase f	
voile m	voile f	

We know all too well that it is difficult to pick up minimal distinctions of this kind in a second language. In some of the pairs and groups given, spelling provides helpful support. Here again, however, it is worth mimicking the experience of the native French-speaker, who will hear such words time and again in contexts which will reinforce the difference. In the following examples, I have provided contexts which may help to entrench the distinctions in your memory. Some

Le bal/la balle

of these are simply typical sequences which emphasise the gender. Others function in French as fixed expressions.

la *foi* chrétienne
le pâté de *foie* gras
Il y avait une *fois*...

On est bien dans sa *peau*
Tu prends un *pot*?

Le *parti* québécois (conservateur)
en grande *partie*

Chacun à son *tour*
Au moyen âge, les grandes *tours* étaient importantes pour la défense
On se rencontre à la *Tour* Eiffel

La nostalgie de la *boue*
Au *bout* de la rue...

Les *moules* marinières sont excellentes
Les bateaux en fibre de verre sont fabriqués au moyen d'un *moule*

Mon (ton, son) *père*
Une *paire* de souliers/gants

Une chemise à *manches* courtes/longues
Jeter le *manche* après la cognée

Pour mettre la table, il faut du *sel*, du poivre, du pain et du beurre
Vous voulez du *sel*?
Faire faire une *selle* spéciale pour son cheval

La grande *voile* du bateau
Le *voile* blanc de la religieuse

Un oeuf à la *coque*
Une *coque* de noix
La *coque* du bateau
Le *coq* de la basse-cour

Les *crêpes* bretonnes sont bonnes à manger
Une robe en *crêpe* blanc

The following children's rhyme, like many such items, not only plays on words in a manner calculated to please the very young, but can also serve as a mnemonic for the difficult set of homophones *foi*, *foie* and *fois* which no native French speaker seems to confuse, but which causes most Anglophones considerable difficulty:

Il était une fois
Un p'tit bonhomme de Foix
Qui vendait du foie
Sur la place Sainte-Foi.
Il se dit: Ma foi,
Puisque j'ai mal au foie,
J'achète cette fois
Une tasse de thé, ma foi,
Boldoflorine, ma foi.

(The rhyme exists in several versions. This a commercial adaptation which includes more instances of the problem words than most. *Boldoflorine* is a commercial name.)

Systematic Homophones

We have already seen that adjectives are freely used to create nouns. Nouns are also used to create adjectives. *Rose* f becomes an adjective, as in *une robe rose*. The adjective *rose* in turn is used as a masculine noun meaning 'the colour pink'. This leads to the existence of a number of series of homophonous pairs. Colour words provide other good examples such as the following:

orange f 'an orange'
orange m 'the colour orange'

groseille f 'red currant'
groseille m 'the colour cherry red'

aubergine f 'aubergine or egg plant'
aubergine m 'the colour aubergine'

Nouns denoting people often have homophonous forms which are masculine or feminine according to the gender of the person denoted. (In traditional usage, the masculine also denotes a person of unknown gender). Examples are:

acrobate	adulte	aéronaute
aide	aristocrate	artiste
automobiliste	bureaucrate	camarade
concierge	cosmonaute	cycliste
démocrate	élève	enfant
enthousiaste	fleuriste	gosse
homicide	hypocrite	nationaliste
royaliste	patriote	sexagénaire
socialiste	syndicaliste	

Une acrobate audacieuse et un acrobate audacieux

Femininising nouns in this way has found much favour, both in France and in Canada, with those looking for elegant ways of writing or speaking in gender-neutral style. The result is that this category is now constantly increasing.

Notice that French speakers are well able to distinguish nouns denoting humans or animals from those denoting inanimates, as well as abstract from concrete. Hence you will find series such as the following, in which animate and inanimate nouns constitute a complex homophonic group and in which gender performs one of the distinguishing functions:

aide f 'help'
aide m 'helper' (male)
aide f 'helper' (female)

garde f 'guard duty'
garde m 'guard' (male)
garde f 'guard' (female)

mort m 'dead person'
mors m 'bit'
mort f 'death'

The number of such groups is again increasing as feminisation of nouns denoting women becomes accepted. In present-day Canada, you could include the series:

critique f 'criticism'
critique m 'critic (male)'
critique f 'critic (female)'

The homophones distinguished by gender, alone or in combination with other factors, help to show why it is important not to ignore the phenomenon of gender in your learning of French.

Activities

(1) Form sentences in which two (or more) homophonous nouns are used. Mark the gender clearly.

Example: Arrivant au bord du fleuve, j'ai attaché le bateau à un petit chêne au moyen d'une grande chaîne.

(2) Find examples of masculine nouns designating humans and ending in consonant plus -*e*. Feminise your noun by changing the determinant. Use your examples in sentences which clearly display their gender.

Example: La juge, consciente de sa responsabilité importante, a attendu le lendemain avant de prononcer le jugement.

Seeing How the Network Operates

In this section, we look at an example of a text such as might well provide reading material for students of French. To this text, I propose to apply a sorting system for noun genders which models approximately the process by which words are sorted as they are acquired by native speakers of French. Some words can be seen as conforming to the rules or tendencies governing a particular category of nouns. Others will be identified as abnormal according to this criterion, in which case they obviously require more attention.

Sample Text

(The nouns presumed to be new to the reader are italicised.)

> Je commence maintenant à penser à un *projet* intéressant pour mes prochaines *vacances*. Cet *été*, j'aimerais faire un beau *voyage* en Ontario dans la *région* exquise des Mille-Iles. On me dit qu'on peut y louer un grand *houseboat* à un prix relativement bas. Il n'est pas indispensable d'avoir de l'*expérience* ni d'avoir passé des *examens* de *navigation*. Mais on n'a pas le *droit* de naviguer sur le *lac*: il faut se limiter au *fleuve*. Ce n'est pourtant pas un petit *ruisseau*, le Saint-Laurent.
>
> Vous pouvez également louer un beau *bateau à voile*, et vous aurez alors l'*autorisation* d'aller partout à condition de revenir le *jour* prévu et à l'*heure* spécifiée. Le *gérant* fera simplement une *sortie* courte avec vous pour évaluer votre *compétence* et pour vous montrer comment lever les *voiles*.
>
> On vous conseille d'acheter à l'avance tout le *matériel* dont vous pourriez avoir besoin en cas d'*accident* ou de mauvais *temps*. Aux *mois* de juillet et d'août, il y aura presque toujours de grands *orages*, et on n'est jamais sûr d'échapper à la *pluie*. Je vais donc acheter de bonnes *ceintures de sauvetage*, une *paire* d'*espadrilles* non-glissantes et un *ciré*. Et, puisque après tout je suis optimiste, un *maillot de bain* de la plus grande *élégance*.

This vocabulary can be sorted as follows:

(1) Animate nouns:

optimiste m or f according to the writer, *gérant* m

(2) Inanimate noun belonging to one of the recognised semantic groups:

été m

(3) Inanimate nouns formed by suffix or conversion:

autorisation f	ceinture f	ciré m
compétence f	élégance f	navigation f
sortie f		

(4) Inanimate compounds:

bateau à voile, masculine like bateau
ceinture de sauvetage, feminine like ceinture
maillot de bain, masculine like maillot

(5) Simple inanimate nouns, the gender of which conforms to the phonetic tendencies:

accident m	droit m	espadrille f
expérience f	jour m	lac m
mois m	orage m	pluie f
projet m	région f	ruisseau m
temps m	vacances f	voyage m

(6) Simple inanimate nouns not conforming to the phonetic tendencies:

fleuve m	heure f	paire f

(7) Simple inanimate nouns having an ending ambiguous as to gender:

houseboat m	matériel m	voile f

All of the nouns given here, except the six in the last two categories, are covered by and conform to one or other of the rules or tendencies we have examined. These six are therefore the ones of which the gender would require special attention.

For difficult cases, there are two indicators which might help you to assign the correct gender. First, the written ending -e is often, but by no means always, associated with the feminine. However, this tendency, at best not a reliable one, is particularly likely to mislead in the case of 'learned' words. Second, the gender of inanimate nouns borrowed from English is likely to be masculine unless the noun has an ending which resembles a French suffix associated with the feminine, such as -ation, -ure.

What I have done here is simply to make explicit the sorting process which, if you assimilate the gender system, it should teach you to perform automatically and without conscious monitoring. It will, however, do so only if you play your part by becoming aware of gender markers in your listening, reading, speaking and writing, and if, like all young French speakers, you learn the genders of the most frequent nouns so well that a gender error becomes unthinkable.

Activities

(1) Look back over your written assignments for the last few months. See what proportion of the mistakes involve gender errors or defective gender marking.

(2) With a partner or as a group, try sorting the nouns involved in the mistakes as has been done here. See what proportion of the mistakes could have been avoided by applying rules you now know.

(3) From the nouns involved in the errors, select those which you use or encounter frequently. Memorise the genders of these nouns by using them in structures which strongly mark genders.

(4) Write about your own travel plan for the next holiday season. Use new vocabulary found in travel brochures. Mark the genders of new words so that they entrench themselves in your memory. Use a thesaurus or a dictionary which provides synonyms to find adjectives emphasising gender.

In Conclusion

We have seen that genders are assigned to French nouns not randomly, as has been said in the past, but according to a network of systems. We can sum up the principal factors at work as follows:

Animate Nouns

(1) Nouns denoting humans are strongly affected by a link between linguistic and biological or sociological gender, as in the case of *garçon* m versus *fille* f.

(ii) Nouns denoting animals are also affected by this link, but less consistently. Those most closely associated with human beings, mostly mammals, are distinguished by sex, the masculine gender usually being assigned to the generic term, as in the series *chat, matou, chatte*. The gender of names for animals which are usually considered to be lower on the scale of living things as seen by humans is more likely to be feminine.

Inanimate Nouns

(1) Simple nouns follow certain phonetic tendencies. For instance, the vast majority of nouns ending in [ʒ] or[ɛ̃] are masculine, as in piège, collège; pain, teint.

(2) Certain nouns of high frequency are governed by a set of semantic rules. Examples are colour terms (*le rouge, le noir*) and names of types of wine (*le champagne, le beaujolais*).

(3) Derived or compound nouns, including technical and 'learned' nouns, are governed by rules related to their structure. For example: nouns formed by the addition of -*ation* are feminine (*cessation, organisation*); those formed from verb plus noun are masculine (*casse-croûte, essuie-glace*).

In order to absorb the gender system into your competence as a speaker and writer of French, you should try to observe the following practices:

(1) Train yourself to listen and look for gender markers.

(2) If you are committing vocabulary to memory, don't neglect to add in the gender of nouns.

(3) Try to mark the genders, when you are speaking or writing, by means of a conspicuous gender marker, or preferably more than one, as in:

le dernier chapitre
le grand chêne
la belle couleur
le paragraphe suivant
cette photo merveilleuse

(4) Accustom yourself to thinking of words as living entities, a great many of which are created from existing meaningful items. When you see or hear a new noun, try to find parallel examples. Can you see how the gender is arrived at? In a good number of cases, the structure should tell you.

(5) If you are confused by two nouns which sound the same, or very similar, try to find familiar expressions containing each of the two problem words which will help you to remember which is which.

(6) Above all, ensure that you routinely get the genders of simple, frequent words right. Once you have decided that gender is important to you, you will be training yourself to listen for clues to gender. Soon you will be able, as all French-speaking children do, to deduce most genders from the context in which a noun is used. Mastering this stage will provide you with the necessary knowledge and habits for dealing with complex nouns, including the technical and 'learned' ones.

Additional Tests

Additional tests are provided on the next two pages to help you to judge your progree towards assigning genders with a high degree of accuracy. Again, you might wish to photocopy the tests before filling in the answers, so as to be able to test yourself again at a later stage.

Test II

crime	( )	raticide	( )	pause-café	( )
catalogue	( )	foie	( )	balcon	( )
pommier	( )	liquide	( )	télé	( )
girafe	( )	triomphe	( )	horloge	( )
bronze	( )	métro	( )	garage	( )
blouse	( )	prune	( )	poème	( )
automne	( )	orangeraie	( )	cave	( )
foi	( )	soif	( )	litre	( )
beauté	( )	thermomètre	( )	âge	( )
rime	( )	apprentissage	( )	appendicite	( )
caféine	( )	problème	( )	prison	( )
téléphone	( )	panthère	( )	radio	( )
radiale	( )	tube	( )	vertu	( )
lune	( )	oxygène	( )	soleil	( )
moustique	( )	horreur	( )	poésie	( )
lave-vaisselle	( )	papier	( )	dimanche	( )
royaume	( )	siège	( )		

The correct answers are on page 64
SCORE_____ DATE _____

Test III

dent	( )	savon	( )	mélancolie	( )
sud	( )	marché	( )	supposition	( )
génie	( )	allure	( )	craie	( )
carton	( )	crème	( )	photo	( )
boisson	( )	allume-gaz	( )	neige	( )
pouls	( )	beurre	( )	pêche	( )
boulangerie	( )	physique	( )	vélo	( )
royaume	( )	arrosoir	( )	vase (mud)	( )
baleine	( )	micro	( )	sida	( )
cygne	( )	platane	( )	chimie	( )
brebis	( )	midi	( )	rêve	( )
ligne	( )	molaire	( )	hydrogène	( )
mille-pattes	( )	golfe	( )	guêpe	( )
préférence	( )	sortie	( )	vingtaine	( )
fleur	( )	type	( )	souris	( )
crabe	( )	parti	( )	coque	( )
TGV	( )	TVA	( )		

The correct answers are on page 65
SCORE_____ DATE_____

Gender Assignment Tests: Correct Answers

Test I

lessive	(f)	idée	(f)	génie	(m)
goutte	(f)	affiche	(f)	machine	(f)
chemin	(m)	luxe	(m)	emploi	(m)
repas	(m)	trou	(m)	vertu	(f)
barbe	(f)	ministère	(m)	film	(m)
école	(f)	piège	(m)	poème	(m)
menace	(f)	temps	(m)	paix	(f)
incendie	(m)	banane	(f)	milieu	(m)
horloge	(f)	queue	(f)	ambulance	(f)
étoffe	(f)	cave	(f)	boutique	(f)
courage	(m)	empire	(m)	mois	(m)
ligne	(f)	faim	(f)	chambre	(f)
plage	(f)	état	(m)	fusil	(m)
acier	(m)	navire	(m)	équipe	(f)
heure	(f)	soupe	(f)	poivre	(m)
marche	(f)	coude	(m)	poche	(f)
feuille	(f)	automobile	(f)	brouillard	(m)
nuit	(f)	date	(f)		

Test II

crime	(m)	raticide	(m)	pause-café	(f)
catalogue	(m)	foie	(m)	balcon	(m)
pommier	(m)	liquide	(m)	télé	(f)
girafe	(f)	triomphe	(m)	horloge	(f)
bronze	(m)	métro	(m)	garage	(m)
blouse	(f)	prune	(f)	poème	(m)
automne	(m)	orangeraie	(f)	cave	(f)
foi	(f)	soif	(f)	litre	(m)
beauté	(f)	thermomètre	(m)	âge	(m)
rime	(f)	apprentissage	(m)	appendicite	(f)
caféine	(f)	problème	(m)	prison	(f)
téléphone	(m)	panthère	(f)	radio	(f)
radiale	(f)	tube	(m)	vertu	(f)
lune	(f)	oxygène	(m)	soleil	(m)
moustique	(m)	horreur	(f)	poésie	(f)
lave-vaisselle	(m)	papier	(m)	dimanche	(m)
royaume	(m)	siège	(m)		

Test III

dent	(f)	savon	(m)	mélancolie	(f)
sud	(m)	marché	(m)	supposition	(f)
génie	(m)	allure	(f)	craie	(f)
carton	(m)	crème	(f)	photo	(f)
boisson	(f)	allume-gaz	(m)	neige	(f)
pouls	(m)	beurre	(m)	pêche	(f)
boulangerie	(f)	physique	(f)	vélo	(m)
royaume	(m)	arrosoir	(m)	vase (mud)	(f)
baleine	(f)	micro	(m)	sida	(m)
cygne	(m)	platane	(m)	chimie	(f)
brebis	(f)	midi	(m)	rêve	(m)
ligne	(f)	molaire	(f)	hydrogène	(m)
mille-pattes	(m)	golfe	(m)	guêpe	(f)
préférence	(f)	sortie	(f)	vingtaine	(f)
fleur	(f)	type	(m)	souris	(f)
crabe	(m)	parti	(m)	coque	(f)
TGV	(m)	TVA	(f)		

A List of Frequent Nouns With Their Genders

The following list includes most of the words given in this book as examples, as well as others which are used frequently in French. Many are included in *le français fondamental* or in vocabulary lists designed for students at the intermediate level. It provides you with a suggested group of words of which you might want to learn the genders very thoroughly. It also provides a quick check-list of important genders for review. The more certain you are of using these words correctly with the proper gender, the closer you will be to assimilating the systems used by Francophone speakers to assign genders with enviable accuracy. Since the gender of nouns designating humans, at least as prescribed by traditional grammar, is usually obvious, they are mostly omitted. Only a sampling of animal names is included: some of the most frequent, and of those whose gender often causes difficulty. The abbreviation Q indicates a word or variation common in Québec.

abattoir m	abeille f	aboiement m
abondance f	abri m	abricot m
absence f	absolu m	abus m
accent m	accident m	accueil m
achat m	acier m	acte m
action f	activité f	actualité f
addition f	adieu m	adjectif m
administration f	admiration f	adresse f
adverbe m	aérodrome m	aéroport m
affaire f	affection f	affiche f
affirmation f	âge m	agneau m
agriculture f	agoraphobie f	agronomie f
aide f	aide-mémoire m	aigle m
aiguille f	aile f	air m
alcool m	aliment m	allée f
alliage m	alliance f	allumette f
allume-gaz m	allure f	alphabet m

altimètre m	aluminium m	ambition f
ambulance f	âme f	amitié f
amour m	ampoule f	an m
ananas m	ancre f	âne m/ânesse f
anémomètre m	ange m	angle m
anglophobie f	angoisse f	animal m
anneau m	année f	anniversaire m
annonce f	anorak m	antiquité f
août m	appareil m	apparence f
appartement m	appareil photo m	appel m
appendectomie f	appendicite f	appétit m
application f	apprentissage m	après-midi m/f
arbre m	ardoise f	argent m
arme f	armée f	armoire f
arrêt m	arrivée f	arrosoir m
art m	article m	artillerie f
ascenseur m	aspect m	aspirine f
assemblée f	assiette f	association f
assurance f	astronautique f	astre m
atelier m	athéisme m	atmosphère f
attaque f	attente f	attention f
attitude f	attrape-mouche m	auberge f
audace f	augmentation f	auto f
autobus m(/f Q)	autocar m	automne m
auto f	automobile f	autorail m
autoroute f	avance f	avantage m
avenue f	averse f	aveu m
aviation f	avion m	avion-citerne m
avis m	avril m	
Bac m	bagage m	bague f
baguette f	baie f	bain m
bal m	balai m	balance f
balcon m	baleine f	balle f
ballon m	banane f	banc m
bande f	bande dessinée f	banlieue f
banque f	bar m	barbe f
barque f	barrage m	barre f

bas m	bas-nylon m	bassin m
bataille f	bataillon m	bateau m
bâtiment m	bâton m	beauté f
bec m	béret m	besogne f
besoin m	bétail m	bête f
beurre m	bibliothèque f	bicyclette f
bien m	bière f	bifteck m
bijou m	bijouterie f	bille f
billet m	biologie f	bise f
blague f	blancheur f	blé m
blessure f	bleu m	bloc m
blouse f	boeuf m	boîte aux lettres f
bois m	boisson f	boîte f
bol m	bonbon m	bonheur m
bonjour m	bonnet m	bonsoir m
bonté f	bord m	botte f
bouche f	boucherie f	bouchon m
boue f	bouillon m	boulangerie f
boule f	boulevard m	bouquet m
bouquin m	bourg m	bourse f
bout m	bouteille f	boutique f
bouton m	boxe f	BQ (bloc québécois) m (Q)
branche f	bras m	brasserie f
bravoure f	brin m	brique f
briquet m	brise-vent m	brochure f
brosse f	brouette f	brouillard m
bruit m	brûlure f	brume f
brun m	buffet m	bulletin m
bureau m	bureau de change m	bureau de poste m
bureau de tabac m	but m	

cabinet m	cachet m	cachette f
cadavre m	cadeau m	cadre m
café m	café crème m	caféine f
cafétéria f	cafetière f	cage f
cahier m	caillou m	caisse f
calcul m	calculateur m	caleçon m
calme m	camélia m	caméra m

camion m	camion à remorque m	camionnette f
camp m	camping m	campagne f
canal m	canard m/cane f	cancer m
canine f	canon m	canot m
cantine f	caoutchouc m	cap m
capitale f	car m	caractère m
carafe f	caravane f	cardiologie f
carnet m	carotte f	carré m
carreau m	carrefour m	carte f
carte routière f	carte postale f	carton m
cas m	casque m	casquette f
casserole f	cassette f	cathédrale f
cause f	cavalerie f	cave f
cégep m (Q)	ceinture f	cendre f
cendrier m	centaine f	centième m
centre m	centigramme m	centimètre m
cercle m	cerf m	cerise f,
cerisier m	certificat m	cerveau m
cervelle f	chagrin m	chaîne f
chaîne stéréo f	chaise f	chambre f
chameau m	champ m	champignon m
championnat m	chance f	changement m
chanson f	chant m	chantier m
chapeau m	char m	char de combat m
charbon m	charcuterie f	charge f
charpente f	charrette f	charrue f
chasse f	chat m/chatte f	château m
chaud m	chaudière f	chauffage m
chaussette f	chaussure f	chaux f
chemin m	cheminée f	chemise f
chêne m	chèque m	chèque de voyage m
cheval m	cheveu m	chèvre f
chien m/chienne f	chiffon m	chiffre m
chimie f	chocolat m	choix m
chômage m	chose f	chou m
chou-fleur m	cidre m	ciel m
cigare m	cigarette f	cigogne f
ciment m	cimetière m	cinéma m

cinq m	cinquantaine f	cinquantième m
cinquième m	circonstance f	cire f
cirque m	ciseaux m	cité f
citron m	citronnier m	civilisation f
clarté f	classe f	claustrophobie f
clé f	climat m	cloche f
clocher m	clou m	club m
cochon m	code m	code postal m
coeur m	coiffure f	coin m
col m	colère f	colis m
collant m	colle f	collection f
collège m	collier m	colline f
combat m	combinaison f	comble m
comédie f	comité m	commencement m
commerce m	commissariat m	commission f
commune f	communisme m	communication f
compagnie f	compartiment m	complément m
complet m	composition f	compte m
compte-gouttes m	comptoir m	concert m
conclusion f	concorde f	concours m
condition f	conditionnel m	conduite f
confiance f	confiture f	confort m
confusion f	congé m	congélateur m
conjonction f	conjugaison f	connaissance f
conscience f	conseil m	conséquence f
consigne f	consonne f	constat m
constitution f	construction f	consulat m
conte m	contrat m	contenu m
conversation f	coq m	coque f
corde f	corne f	corps m
correspondance f	corsage m	costume m
côte f	côté m	coteau m
coton m	cou m	coude m
couleur f	couloir m	coup m
coup de soleil m	cour f	courage m
courbe f	couronne f	cours m
course f	couteau m	coutume f
couture f	couvent m	couvercle m

couvert m	couverture f	crabe m
craie f	crainte f	crâne m
cravate f	crayon m	crédit m
crème f	crémerie f	crêpe m
crêpe f	cri m	crime m
crise f	crochet m	croisement m
croissant m	croix f	croûte f
croyance f	cruche f	crudités f
cuiller f	cuiller à soupe f	cuir m
cuisine f	cuisinière f	cuisse f
cuivre m	culotte f	culture f
curiosité f	cuvette f	cyclisme m
cygne m	cystite f	

danger m	danse f	date f
débat m	début m	décembre m,
décision f	déclaration f	décoration f
défaut m	défense f	degré m,
déjeuner m	délai m	délicatesse f
demande f	demeure f	demi m
dent f	dentifrice m	départ m
département m	dépense f	déplacement m
dépôt m	descente f	description f
désert m	désir m	désordre m
dessert m	dessin m	dessous m
dessus m	destin m	destination f
détail m	déterminatif m	dette f
Deug m	deuil m	deuxième m
devant m	déviation f	devoir m,
dévouement m	diable m	diagramme m
dictionnaire m	différence f	difficulté f
dimanche m	diminution f	dîner m
diplôme m	direction f	disco m
discothèque f	discours m	discussion f
disposition f	dispute f	disque m
distance f	distraction f	distribution f
divan m	division f	divorce m
dix m	dix-huit m	dix-huitième m

dixième m	dizaine f	doigt m
domaine m	dommage m	dortoir m
dos m	douane f	double m
douceur f	douche f	doute m
douzaine f	douze m	drap m
drapeau m	drap-housse m	droit m
droite f	durée f	dureté f
eau f	eau minérale f	échange m
échec m	échelle f	éclair m
éclat m	école f	économie f
écorce f	écran m	écriture f
écurie f	édifice m	éducation f
effet m	effort m	égalité f
église f	égout m	élection f
électricité f	électrophone m	élégance f
élément m	éléphant m	élevage m
émission f	émotion f	empire m
emplacement m	emploi m	emploi du temps m
emprunt m	encre f	endroit m
énergie f	enfance f	engagement m
ennui m	enseignement m	ensemble m
enterrement m	entrée f	entreprise f
entretien m	enveloppe f	envie f
environs m	épaule f	épi m
épicerie f	épingle f	éponge f
époque f	équipage m	équipe f
érable m	erreur f	escadre f
escalier m	espace m	espèce f
espérance f	espoir m	esprit m
essai m	essence f	est m
estime f	estomac m	étable f
établissement m	étage m	étain m
état m	été m	étendue f
éternité f	étoffe f	étoile f
être m	étude f	événement m
évier m	examen m	excursion f
excuse f	exécution f	exemple m

exercice m

exigence f

existence f

expérience f

explication f

explosion f

exportation f

exposition f

express m

expression f

extérieur m

extrême m

extrémité f

fable f

fabrique f

fac f

face f

facilité f

façon f

facteur m

facture f

faculté f

faible m

faiblesse f

faim f

fait m

famille f

farine f

fatigue f

faute f

fauteuil m

faux f

faveur f

félicitations f

fenêtre f

fente f

fer m

ferme f

fête f

feu m

feuillage m

feuille f

février m

ficelle f

fiche f

fiche-renvoi m

fièvre f

figure f

fil m

filet m

film m

fin f

fin de semaine f

finances f

fleur f

fleuve m

flot m

flotte f

foi f

foie m

foin m

foire f

fois f

folie f

fonction f

fond m

fontaine f

football m

force f

forêt f

forge f

forme f

fortune f

fossé m

foule f

four m

four aux microondes m

fourche f

fourchette f

fourmi f

fourneau m

fourrure f

fraîcheur f

frais m pl

fraise f

fraisier m

framboise f

franc m

fraternité f

fraude f

frein m

frites f

froid m

fromage m

frontière f

fruit m

fruitier m

fruits de mer m

fumée f

fusée f

fusil m

futur m

futurisme m

gant m

garage m

garde f

gare f	gare routière f	gastronomie f
gâteau m	gauche f	gaz m
gaze f	génie m	genou m
genre m	géographie f	gerbe f
gibier m	gilet m	girafe f
glace f	gloire f	golf m
golfe m	gomme f	gorge f
goût m	goûter m	goutte f
gouvernail m	grâce f	grain m
graine f	graisse f	grammaire f
gramme m	grandeur f	grange f
grappe f	gratte-ciel m	grêle f
grenier m	grenouille f	grève f
griffe f	grippe f	grosseur f
groupe m	guêpe f	guerre f
gueule f	guichet m	guide m
guitare f		

habit m	habitude f	hache f
haie f	haine f	halte f
haricot m	hasard m	haut m
hauteur f	hélicoptère m	hépatite f
herbe f	herbicide m	heure f
hippodrome m	hirondelle f	histoire f
hiver m	hockey m	homicide m/f
honneur m	honte f	hôpital m
horizon m	horloge f	horreur f
hors d'oeuvre m	hospitalité f	hôtel m
hôtel de ville m	houblon m	houx f
houille f	huile f	huit m
huitième m	humanité f	humeur f
humidité f	hydrothérapie f	hypermarché m

idée f	idéal m	identité f
île f	illustration f	image f
imagination f	imitation f	immensité f
immobilité f	imparfait m	impatience f
importance f	importation f	impossible m

impôt m — impression f — imprimante f
imprimerie f — incendie m — incident m
incisive f — inconvénient m — indépendance f
indicatif m — indication f — indifférence f
industrie f — infanterie f — infinitif m
infirmerie f — infirmité f — influence f
information f — initiative f — injure f
inondation f — inquiétude f — insecte m
insecticide m — inspection f — instant m
instinct m — instruction f — instrument m
intelligence f — intention f — intérêt m
intérieur m — interjection f — intervalle m
intestin m — introduction f — invention f
invitation f — ivresse f

jalousie f — jambe f — jambon m
janvier m — jardin m — jaune m
je ne sais quoi m — jeu m — jeudi m
jeunesse f — joie f — joue f
jouet m — jour m — journal m
journée f — jugement m — juillet m
juin m — jument f — jupe f
jus m — jus de fruit m — justice f

képi m — kilo m — kilogramme m
kilomètre m

labo m — laboratoire m — lac m
laideur f — laine f — lait m
lame f — lampe f — langage m
langue f — lapin m/lapine f — largeur f
larme f — lavabo m — lave-vaisselle m
leçon f — lecture f — légume m
lenteur f — lessive f — lettre f
lèvre f — liberté f — librairie f
lieu m — lièvre m — ligne f
lime f — limite f — limonade f
linge m — lion m/lionne f — liquide m

liste f	lit m	litre m
littérature f	livre m	livre f
location f	locomotive f	logement m
loi f	longueur f	louche f
loup m/louve f	loupe f	loyer m
lueur f	lumière f	lundi m
lune f	lunettes f	lutte f
luxe m	lycée m	

machine f	mâchoire f	magasin m
magazine m	magnétophone m	mai m
maille f	maillet m	maillot de bain m
main f	mairie f	maison f
mal m	maladie f	malentendu m
malheur m	malle f	manche m
manche f	mandat m	manif f
manifestation f	manoeuvre f	manteau m
marais m	marbre m	marchandise f
marche f	marché m	mardi m
marée f	mariage m	marine f
marmite f	marque f	marron m
mars m	marteau m	masse f
mât m	match m	matelas m
matériel m	mathématiques f	matière f
matin m	matinée f	mécanique f
médecine f	médicament m	mégaphone m
mélange m	melon m	mémoire m
mémoire f	menace f	ménage m
mensonge m	menu m	mer f
mercerie f	mercredi m	mérite m
merveille f	mesure f	métal m
métallurgie f	météo f	météorologie f
méthode f	métier m	mètre m
métro m	meuble m	meurtre m
micro m	microphone m	microscope m
midi m	miel m	milieu m
milliard m	millième m	milligramme m
millier m	millimètre m	million m

mine f	mine de sel f	minerai m
ministère m	minuit m	minute f
miracle m	misère f	missile m
mission f	mode m	mode f
modèle m	modestie f	module m
mois m	moisson f	moitié f
molaire f	moment m	monde m
monnaie f	mont m	montagne f
montre f	monument m	moral m
morale f	morceau m	mors m
morphine f	mort f	mot m
moteur m	moto f	motocyclette f
mouche f	mouchoir m	moue f
moule m	moule f	moulin m
mousse f	moustique m	mouton m
mouvement m	moyen m	moyenne f
multiplication f	mur m	mûre f
murmure m	musée m	musique f
mystère m	mythe m	

nage f	naissance f	nappe f
natation f	nation f	nationalité f
nature f	naturel m	naufrage m
navet m	navigation f	navire m
nécessaire m	nécessité f	neige f
nerf m	nettoyage m	neuf m
neutre m	neuvième m	nez m
nickel m	nid m	Noël m
noir m	noix f	nom m
nombre m	nord m	note f
nourriture f	nouvelle f	novembre m
nuage m	nuit f	numéro m
nylon m		

objet m	obligation f	obscurité f
observation f	obstacle m	obus m
occasion f	occident m	océan m
octobre m	odeur f	odorat m

oeil m — oeuf m — oeuvre f
oie f — oignon m — oiseau m
olive f — olivier m — omelette f
ombre f — ongle m — onze m
onzième m — opéra m — opération f
opinion f — opposition f — or m
orage m — orange f — oranger m
orchestre m — ordinateur m — ordonnance f
ordre m — oreille f — oreiller m
organe m — orge f — orgueil m
orient m — origine f — ornement m
orthographe f — os m — ouest m
ouïe f — ours m/ourse f — outil m
ouverture f — ouvrage m

page f — paie f — pain m
paille f — paire f — paix f
palais m — panier m — panne f
pansement m — pantalon m — panthère f
pantoufle f — papeterie f — papier m
papillon m — paquebot m — paquet m
parachute m — paradis m — parapluie m
parc m — pardessus m — pardon m
paresse f — parfum m — parfumerie f
parking m — parlement m — parole f
part f — parquet m — partage m
parti m — participe m — partie f
pas m — passage m — passeport m
passe-temps m — passion f — pastille f
pâte f — pâté m — patience f
pâtisserie f — patinoire f — patrie f
patron m — patte f — pâturage m
pause f — pause-café f — pauvreté f
pavillon m — paiement m — paye f
pays m — paysage m — péage m
peau f — pêche f — péché m
pédale f — peigne f — peine f
peinture f — pelle f — pendule f

péniche f	pénicilline f	pension f
pension complète f	pente f	Pentecôte f
perche f	péril m	période f
périodique m	périscope m	permission f
perroquet m	personnage m	personne f
personnel m	perte f	petitesse f
pétrole m	peu m	peuple m
peuplier m	peur f	phare m
pharmacie f	phono m	phonographe m
photo f	photographie f	phrase f
physique f	physiothérapie f	piano m
pie f	pièce f	pièce de théâtre f
pièce d'identité f	pied m	piège m
pierre f	piété f	pieu m
pigeon m	pile f	pilule f
pin m	pince f	pinceau m
pincettes f	pioche f	pipe f
pique-nique m	piquet m	piqûre f
piscine f	pistolet m	pitié f
placard m	place f	plafond m
plage f	plaie f	plaine f
plainte f	plaisir m	plan m
planche f	planche à voile f	plancher m
planète f	plante f	plaque f
plastique m	plat m	plat du jour m
plateau m	plâtre m	plein m
pli m	plomb m	pluie f
plume f	pluriel m	plus-que parfait m
pneu m	poche f	poêle m
poêle f	poème m	poésie f
poids m	poignée f	poignet m
poil m	poing m	point m
pointe f	pointure f	poire f
poireau m	poirier m	poison m
poisson m	poitrine f	poivre m
police f	politesse f	politique f
polka f	pollution f	pommade f
pomme f	pomme de terre f	pommier m

pompe f	pont m	pop m
population f	porc m	port m
porte f	portefeuille m	porte-monnaie m
portrait m	position f	possessif m
possibilité f	poste (de radio) m	poste f
pot m	potage m	poubelle f
pouce m	poudre f	poule f
poulet m	poumon m	poupée f
pourboire m	poussière f	poussin m
poutre f	pouvoir m	PQ (parti québécois) m
prairie f	pratique f	pré m
précaution f	précédent m	précis m
préférence f	prénom m	préposition f
présence f	présidence f	presse f
pressoir m	prétexte m	preuve f
prière f	principe m	printemps m
priorité f	prison f	prix m
problème m	procédé m	procès m
production f	profession f	profit m
profondeur f	programme m	progrès m
proie f	projectile m	projet m
promenade f	promesse f	pronom m
prononciation f	propagande f	propos m
proposition f	propreté f	propriété f
protège-dents m	proverbe m	province f
provision f	prudence f	prune f
prunier m	psychologie f	psychothérapie f
public m	publicité f	puissance f
puits m	pull m	pullover m
punition f	purée f	pureté f
pyjama m		

quai m	qualité f	quantité f
quarantième m	quart m	quartier m
quatorze m	quatorzième m	quatre m
question f	queue f	quinine f
quinzaine f	quinze m	quinzième m
quotidien m		

race f	racine f	radiale f
radiateur m	radio f	radiographie f
rage f	raisin m	raison f
rame f	rang m	rapport m
rasoir m	rassemblement m	rat m/rate f
râteau m	raticide m	rayon m
rayonne f	réalité f	réception f
réchaud m	recherche f	récipient m
récit m	réclame f	récolte f
récompense f	récréation f	recrue f
rectangle m	reçu m	réduction f
réforme f	réfrigérateur m	refuge m
refus m	regard m	régime m
régiment m	région f	règle f
règlement m	règne m	regret m
rein m	relation f	religion f
remarque f	remède m	remerciement m
renard m	rendez-vous m	renseignement m
rentrée f	réparation f	repas m
repentir m	réponse f	repos m
représentation f	reproche m	république f
réseau m	réserve f	résistance f
respect m	ressemblance f	restaurant m
reste m	résultat m	retard m
retour m	retraite f	réunion f
rêve m	réveil m	revenu m
révolution f	revue f	rez-de-chaussée f
richesse f	rideau m	rien m
rime f	rince-doigts m	rire m
risque m	rivage m	rive f
rivière f	riz m	rizière f
robe f	robinet m	rocher m
rôle m	roman m	rond m
ronde f	rose m	rose f
roseau m	rossignol m	roue f
rouleau m	rouge m	roux m
roulette f	route f	ruche f
rue f	ruine f	ruisseau m

ruse f

sable m	sabot m	sac m
sac à main m	sac de couchage m	sagesse f
saison f	salade f	salaire m
saleté f	salière f	salle f
salle de bains f	salon m	salopette f
salut m	samedi m	sandale f
sandwich m	sang m	sanglier m
santé f	sapin m	sardine f
satisfaction f	saucisse f	saucisson m
saut m	savon m	scandale m
scène f	scie f	science f
scierie f	sculpture f	séance f
seau m	seconde f	secours m
secrétaire m	section f	sécurité f
sein m	seize m	seizième m
séjour m	sel m	selle f
semailles f	semaine f	semelle f
semence f	sens m	sensation f
sentier m	sentinelle f	sentiment m
sept m	septembre m	septième m
série f	serpent m	serrure f
service m	service compris m	serviette f
seuil m	sève f	sexe m
sexologie f	shampooing m	siècle m
siège m	sifflement m	sifflet m
signal m	signature f	signe m
silence m	singe m	sirop m
situation f	six m	sixième m
ski m	slip m	société f
soie f	soif f	soin m
soir m	soirée f	sol m
soleil m	solitude f	somme m
somme f	sommeil m	sommet m
somnifère m	son m	sort m
sorte f	sortie f	sou m
souci m	souffle m	soulier m

soupe f	soupière f	source f
sourire m	souris f	sous-sol m
soustraction f	soutien-gorge m	spécialité f
spectacle m	spermicide m	sport m
stade m	station f	station-service f
statue f	statut m	steak m
style m	stylo m	subjonctif m
substance f	succès m	sucre m
sud m	suite f	sujet m
supplément m	supposition f	sûreté f
surface f	surprise f	syndicat m
système m		

tabac m	table f	tableau m
tablier m	tache f	tâche f
taille f	talent m	talon m
tape f	tarif m	tasse f
taureau m	taxe f	taxi m
taxonomie f	technique f	teinturerie f
télé f	télégramme m	télégraphe m
téléphone m	télescope m	téléviseur m
télévision f	témoignage m	température f
tempête f	temple m	temps m
tenailles f	tendresse f	tennis m
tente f	tenue f	terme m
termite m	terrain m	terrasse f
terre f	terreur f	testament m
tête f	texte m	thé m
théâtre m	thermomètre m	TGV m
ticket m	tiers m	tige f
tigre m	timbre m	timbre-quittance m
tire-bouchon m	tissage m	tissu m
titre m	toile f	toilettes f
toit m	tôle f	tomate f
tombe f	ton m	tondeuse f
tonneau m	tonnerre m	tort m
total m	tour m	tour f
tourisme m	trace f	tracteur m

traduction f	train m	trait m
traité m	traitement m	tranche f
transistor m	transport m	travail m
travers m	treize m	treizième m
trente m	trentième m	trésor m
triangle m	tribunal m	tricot m
trois m	troisième m	tronc m
trottoir m	trou m	trouble m
troupe f	troupeau m	truc m
tube m	tuile f	tuyau m
type m		

union f	unité f	université f
usage m	usine f	ustensile m
utilité f		

vacances f	vache f	va-et-vient m
vague f	vaisseau m	vaisselle f
valeur f	valise f	vallée f
vallon m	vanille f	vapeur f
variété f	veau m	vedette f
véhicule m	veille f	veine f
vélo m	vélodrome m	vélomoteur m
velours m	vendanges f pl	vendredi m
vengeance f	vent m	vente f
ventre m	ver m	verbe m
verger m	vermifuge m	verre m
verrou m	vers m	vert m
verticale f	vertu f	veste f
veston m	vêtement m	viande f
vice m	victime f	victoire f
vide m	vie f	vieillesse f
vigne f	vigueur f	village m
ville f	vin m	vingt m
vingtaine f	vingtième m	vinaigre m
violence f	violette f	violon m
visage m	viscose f	virile f
vitesse f	vitre f	vitrine f

vocabulaire m	voeu m	voie f
voile m	voile f	voiture f
voix f	vol m	volonté f
volume m	vote m	voyage m
voyelle f	vue f	
wagon m	w.c. m	weekend m
yaourt m		
zèbre m	zéro m	zone f

Bibliography

The following references document the research on gender to which allusions are made in the text and on which the learning method presented here is based:

Surridge, M.E. and Lessard G. (1984) Pour une prise de conscience du genre grammatical. *Canadian Modern Language Review* 41 (1), 43–52.
Surridge, M.E. (1985) Le genre grammatical des composés en français. *Canadian Journal of Linguistics* 30 (3), 247–71.
Surridge, M.E. (1986) Genre grammatical et dérivation lexicale en français. *Canadian Journal of Linguistics* 31 (3), 267–84.
Surridge, M.E. (1989a) Grammaire et phylogenèse: le genre des animés [-humain] en français. *Alfa (Actes de langue française et de linguistique de l'université Dalhousie)* 2, 120–42.
Surridge, M.E. (1989b) Le facteur sémantique dans l'attribution du genre aux inanimés en français. *Canadian Journal of Linguistics* 34 (1), 1–27.
Surridge, M.E. (1989c) Le genre grammatical en français fondamental: données de base pour l'enseignement et l'apprentissage. *Canadian Modern Language Review* 45 (4), 664–74.
Tucker, R., Rigault A.A. and Lambert, W.R. (1970) Le genre grammatical des substantifs en français: analyse statistique et étude psycholinguistique. In A. Graur *et al.* (eds) *Actes du Xe congrès des linguistes.* Bucarest: Editions de l'Académie de la république socialiste de Roumanie.
Tucker, G.R., Lambert, W.E. and Rigault, A.A. (1977) *The French Speaker's Skill with Grammatical Gender: An Example of Rule-governed Behavior.* The Hague/Paris: Mouton.

A summary of information now available about gender in French is provided in:

Surridge, M.E. (1993) Gender assignment in French: The hierarchy of rules and the chronology of acqusition. *International Review of Applied Linguistics* XXXI/2, 77–95.

A valuable book on gender in general which provides a theoretical overview is:

Corbett, G. (1991) *Gender.* Cambridge: Cambridge University Press.